Balancing the Stones

Balancing the Stones

Mystical Writings to Wake Up Your Soul

Stephanie Acello

Balancing the Stones:
Mystical Writings to Wake Up Your Soul
Heart Writing Series

Published by One Tone Publications, Colorado

ISBN: 978-1-7328533-1-7

Spiritual / Mystical Poetry / Meditations/ Contemplations

Editor: Bobby Haas
Cover design: Victoria Wolf/Stephanie Acello
Layout design: Andrea Costantine
Consultant: Polly Letofsky
Author photo: Sylvia Hooper

This book is printed in the United States of America.

One Tone
PUBLICATIONS

To my son, teachers, authors, mentors, family, and friends of past and present who inspired me through support and contrast. And of course, to my animal gurus who share their wisdom and authenticity daily.

ACKNOWLEDGMENTS

I am deeply grateful for the following people for their assistance, inspiration, encouragement, and guidance: Bobby Haas, my editor; Andrea Costantine, my book layout designer; Victoria Wolf, my cover designer; Polly Letofsky for her guidance and Sylvia Hooper who offered to take my author photo.

And a special nod of gratitude to my family and friends who inspire me on a daily basis. Also, sincere thanks to my writing group for keeping me on track and accountable for my writing.

I must also acknowledge the subtleties of life that allow me to have a peek into the mystical: the soft caress of the breeze on my face, the warmth of the sun on my back, the coolness of the snow, and the magnificent creatures that share my life.

TABLE OF CONTENTS

Introduction	ix
How to Use the Sacred Moment Contemplations	xiv
Part 1 - Inhale	1
1. Be the World You Want to Live In	3
2. Thoughts Before Matter	23
3. Dance your Dance	43
4. Be True to Truth	63
5. The Future is Now	85
6. Follow Heart's Direction	105
Part 2 - Exhale	125
7. The Cocoon of Illusion	127
8. The Shadow is That which is Blocking the Light	149
9. Life's Dream	171
10. The Eyes Do Not See	193
11. Mystical Movement	215
12. Butterfly Emerging	235
Closing	257
Glossary	258

INTRODUCTION

*Open the Door
and meet yourself on the other side*

Balancing the Stones: Mystical Writings to Wake Up Your Soul
is the second book in the *Heart Writing Series*. *Heart Writings*
are mystical and spiritual insights that reflect the essence of life
and attempt to communicate the message of Heart and Soul
into language. And most importantly, these writings help you
reconnect with your Inner Being. The pace of the outside world
is moving very quickly, bringing a bombardment of so much
false information on how the world operates. The demands are
increasing and the peace is decreasing. The deep yearning for
love and joy within us all is knocking on humanity's Door—a
Door only you can open.

Humanity is going through a metamorphosis: we are realizing
change is merely a surface modulation of the same perception
and it is not enough to bring balance to the world and to
individual circumstances. Instead, what is required and needed
is *transformation*: a dramatic shift in perception, consciousness,
and action. The main focus of change is on the outer world
and the temporary—*with a fleeting essence*. The main focus of
transformation is on the Inner Being and the eternal—*with an
enduring essence*.

Humanity, collectively and individually, is in the midst of a
conscious evolution, an awakening to our full potential and the
insight into the nature of existence. The universe is expanding
and all of life, including you, are a part of it—nothing can stop it.
The experience of a conscious evolution includes an *involution*
or a turning inwards for Self-discovery. A discovery revealing
the perception of the outer world is a *direct reflection* of the
contents of our minds, embodied feelings, and belief systems.
This major awareness will require impeccable courage to expose
your True Self from the depths of your Beingness. The peace,
love, kindness, and balance we crave in the world must start
with each one of us. The responsibility is in our hands, like it or

not. *Balancing the Stones* presents the opportunity to begin this shift of perception by offering universal and mystical insights to connect and reestablish your relationship with your True Self.

The mystical realm I am referring to is the realm where the Unity and Oneness of existence is experienced. It is where the finite and infinite meet, mortality and immortality weave together, real and unreal dance, human and spirit kiss, and the inner and outer worlds meld. This realm of Oneness underlies and intertwines within all of existence. It is the realm where All meets in Unity. I consider myself a mystic poet because I attempt to communicate, through the *Heart Writings,* experiential glimpses into the mystery and wonder of life's process. A mystic seeks to engage in Unity and delves deeply and profoundly in the mysterious essence of nature—*an experience available to everyone.* Life is indeed a mystery: once acknowledged, the mystery becomes your guide and teacher.

The *Heart Writings* do not follow conventional written rules: they are uncensored communication from the frequency of Heart and Soul, exposing the Inner Secrets and Knowledge of the Mystical Realm that we all yearn to know. These messages or *infusions* bypass both ego and thoughts to a higher vibrational awareness of Eternal Source and Creative Intelligence, which underlies the whole order of existence. It is a vibrational awareness that is everyone's birthright.

When in alignment with Eternal Source, information does not come from the thinking realm, it comes from the receiving realm—receiving awareness from the expansive perspective of life. To emphasize and honor this awareness, some of the words are capitalized and italicized. When a large section of a *Heart Writing* is italicized, it represents a Receiving Block of information or download of Direct Perception. Also, for a deeper comprehension of the writings, a glossary is added at the end of the book to clarify selected words and terms used in the writings.

The *Heart Writings* are be read slowly and deliberately to yourself, quietly or out loud; then take a moment to contemplate the writing you just read. You may even want to read it over again. The *Heart Writings* are from the vibration of Eternal Source and speak the universal language that touches the human spirit within us all, revealing the mystical magnificence of Life.

In addition to the *Heart Writings,* each chapter includes a *Sacred Moment Contemplation* that offers an opportunity to contemplate by inquiry. Inquiry and contemplation require deep reflective thought: an unfolding process to bring forth awareness and insight.

In my mid-twenties, I was in a yoga ashram, a spiritual community, where I practiced the four main paths of yoga: Bhakti (devotion), Karma (action), Raja (eight steps or limbs of practice and self-discipline) and Jnana Yoga. Jnana Yoga is acquiring wisdom and knowledge by the process of discrimination of what is real and not real through inquiry. It is an intensive practice of sorting life's experiences by saying: *neti neti—not this, not this—* and eventually saying: if *not this,* then *what is?*

What is real? Jnana Yoga uses the mind to inquire into its own nature and transcend the mind's identification with the ego and thoughts. My active Gemini mind is always questioning and contemplating. And through the practice of Jnana Yoga, I began to write down and record the insights that I was experiencing. The insights bypassed my personal mind and went directly to Heart... hence the *Heart Writings.*

The yogis are aware that Jnana Yoga, along with meditation and mindfulness, begins opening channels of awareness to experience *Sat Chit Ananda*—existence, knowledge, and bliss—all happening simultaneously. Through inquiry and contemplation, the mystical and spiritual realm of Consciousness becomes available.

The *Sacred Moment Contemplations* at the end of each chapter include simple activities inquiring into the nature of Self. These simple activities stir deep reflective thought to connect with your Inner Being in just a few moments. Contemplation, inquiry, and questioning are important steps to allow your True Self to come forth. If you want to incorporate simple meditations as well, *Pour Me Another Cup: Mystical Writings to Illuminate Your Soul,* my first published book of *Heart Writings,* has quick and simple *Sacred Moment Meditations* at the end of each chapter.

Balancing the Stones is a unique book to uplift and align with your higher consciousness. I always envisioned the book by the reader's meditation station, on the nightstand by the bed, on the coffee table, on the work desk, or anywhere that allows for easy access. This book accommodates your time and desire to unite with your Inner Being by just turning to any page or section, reading the *Heart Writing,* and allowing the shift to take hold immediately—a shift that will begin to open the Door of Insight and Knowledge.

The surface of the world is similar to the ocean's waves, reflecting the uncertainty and transient nature of physical existence. However, the messages of the *Heart Writings* remain in the still deep waters of the everlasting nature of the eternal, unaffected by the surface of uncertainty—*in it, but not of it.*

The world is balancing on a delicate pivot
One swift wind can move it in either direction
Be the force behind the wind
blowing in both directions equally
to keep the precise balance of Insight

HOW TO USE
THE SACRED MOMENT CONTEMPLATIONS

Each chapter focuses and communicates an insight from a higher vibration of consciousness. At the end of each chapter, a *Sacred Moment Contemplation* is included. The contemplations offer an opportunity to encourage inquiry for a deeper understanding of the chapter's subject—within minutes. Keeping a journal close by would be beneficial.

Sacred Moment Contemplation guidelines:

1. The *Sacred Moment Contemplations* are to be used after you read one or more *Heart Writings*. They can also be used independently.
2. Find a comfortable, quiet, and distraction-free area.
3. Sit on a chair, with your back relaxed and straight, with both feet on the floor or lay down on the floor, couch, or bed (try not to fall asleep). You can also sit cross-legged in a yoga lotus position.
4. Read the *Sacred Moment* on the chapter's subject at least once.
5. Next, read the *Sacred Moment Contemplation* and follow the directions for contemplating the question and the journal entry.
6. The contemplations are a great way to start the day. However, they can be done at any time or any number of times.
7. Most importantly, have fun!

Stacking stones is an art

Balancing the stones depends on the connection
where the stones barely touch

Living a life is an art
It is a fine-tuned balancing affair
Between heaven and earth
Between human and spirit
Between finite and infinity

We belong to both
But live in the connection where they barely touch

Once found
the balancing affair becomes a love affair

PART 1

INHALE

Every aspect of life is blanketed within the Divine Field
speaking the holy and sacred language of Love's vibration

1

BE THE WORLD
YOU WANT TO LIVE IN

The world springs from perception

What do you want from the world?

The world holds nothing
It looks to you
to fill the space

If you want peace
be peaceful
If you want harmony
sing sweet music
If you want generosity
be generous
If you want acceptance
be accepting
If you want tolerance
be tolerant
If you want kindness
be kind
If you want to be heard
listen
If you want love
be loving

It is not a difficult task
The world's existence depends on you
It gets its breath from you
Take a deep breath and breathe out slowly
from your Eternal Beingness

And Be the world
you want to live in

The emergence of a new world
springs from the evolution
of new beliefs

Feel your True Essence
and know where experience originates

Evolution turns inward
and transforms into involution

The inner kingdoms
are the landscapes of the world

The Inner and Outer
have no distinction

Open your eyes
and see with a new Vision

∽⧢∾

Life is a moment
A moment only
Living in the Now

We look for more time
by rushing through the moments
Thinking it will create more moments
This is defective thinking

Moving with urgent haste
leaves nothing
Not even a memory of experience
No story to share

Skating on the surface
and not knowing what lies beneath

Stay within the moment
time is asleep
Presenting the opportunity
to awaken the timeless Essence
of endless moments
Embracing the secrets of eternity

Dive deep in the waters of life
Moment by moment
Totally absorbed

When you come up for air
is the time to
share your story

∽

Being in joy
is the best you can offer the world
It gathers momentum for joy to magnify

The world is not an entity of its own
It reflects the collective entity of humanity
The ancient scrolls confirm this

The world looks for energetic connections
Negative produces more negative
Positive produces more positive
All without judgment

We start a fire
touch it and get burned
And blame the fire for the pain

Ignorance of the world operates the same
Ignoring the obvious

We hold on to
negative and hateful thoughts
creating hurtful circumstances
We experience the circumstances and get burned
And blame the world for the pain

The mystery is about to be revealed
The finger is always pointing to us

When this occurs
who are we going to blame?

Where is the world?

We speak of it
as though it is something real
something unchanging
But where is it?

The common belief
is that the world we sense
is something separate
and outside of ourselves
Including all encounters with
living beings and events
objects and circumstances

This is the cosmic illusion

Believing what we sense
and encounter in the world
is born from the world

In actuality
what we sense and encounter in the world
is born from the images from the
vibration of thoughts and beliefs
we focused on

Our images are projected on the world's screen
reflecting Life's Living Picture

The world does not have the ability to form its own image
Its vocation is to reflect

This is the Great Shift
of awareness and consciousness that is rising
Revealing the creation of the world
is in our hands

We must hold the world like a delicate baby
with love and tolerance
Giving wise direction

Taking full responsibility of its Becoming

Where is the world?

It lives within the illusive dream of impermanence
A mist made from
the frequencies of *belief-vibrations*
A changing perception that lives within us all

Witnessed by the
changeless Eye of Eternal Source

Stand on the summit
and be the Light the world is seeking

As the sun vanishes into the horizon
sound and movement gradually come to a halt

In the darkness
the quiet is deafening
Radiating Light from the One Heart
for all to see

Arms outstretched
allowing the connection to All
with no interference from fear

Love with all your Heart
not your mind
and everything will make sense

DIVINE OBSERVATION ON PERCEPTION

A woman was complaining to a friend about a neighbor who lives across the street. She spoke of how she waves hello every morning to the neighbor, and he never waves back.

"I have been waving to him for weeks, and he never acknowledges me. I am sick of it, this man is a tyrant and rude," the woman grunted.

She became angrier and angrier each morning. She started to fume because she was thinking the worst and taking it personally. She was ready for a fight.

"I will not say hello or wave any longer," she said to herself, as she glared at him with squinting eyes. "If he ever comes here, I will spit on him," and she proceeded to mimic spitting on the ground.

She never did wave again or make eye contact with the neighbor and kept to herself until her death.

WISDOM SPEAKS

The woman was quick to make a judgment
on someone's character and taking it as a personal attack
She kept hostilities within her
creating a story of falsehood
Lost in her illusion of perception

The man did not wave back because he could not see her
He was blind
not being able to see from his eyes
However
she had the worst kind of blindness
not being able to see from her Heart

The stability of the outside world
is a fragile happening

A delicate breeze can push it
in one direction or the other
Lifting the veil or slamming the fort gate shut

Sometimes
I look at the world and
see so much meaning
without question

Other times
I look at the world and
question its meaning

Once you realize atoms want to serve
direct them with keen focus and love

We live in two worlds
The outer world and the inner world

The outer world is the physicality we sense
The inner world is where its perception lives
Alongside your True Self

The outside world is a vibrational instrument of atoms
playing the musical composition of thoughts and beliefs
Given from the breath of humanity
The world is not equipped to create its own music

Can a flute play by itself?

The flute is an instrument
held in your hands
Music or noise can be played
from the breath given

The world is a delicate instrument
held in your hands
Music or noise can be played
from the breath given

The breath of harmony and love
or
discord and fear

To realize and know Universal Spirit
one first has to realize and know one's own Spirit

One's Spirit is an extension
of Universal Spirit

Embrace your Spirit
and dance with the Universe
to the music of Absorption

Knowing
That which moves the Universe
moves you

The vibration is so fine
it bypasses humanness

Once the connection is made
your perspective changes radically
from limited to limitless

Personal self melding with Absolute Self
Seeing from the Eye of the Eternal

You still eat pizza
and your actions may appear
to be the same to others
However
your actions are not yours anymore

⚮

SACRED REFLECTION

Where is the world, we all speak of? Can it be touched?
Can it be held in our hands?

The world is comparable to the blue sky

We see the sky every day
We speak about it
We look up and admire it

But try to
find the blue or where the sky begins and ends
is an impossible task

We all want to change the world
Create a world that is safe and fair
kind and loving

Some feel it is done through service
or through the laws of the land and religion
However
these are categories of moral concepts
Man-made principles and dogma
A temporary fix

You cannot help and serve
all the starving and homeless
You cannot change every law
to have justice for all
You cannot help by forcing beliefs
of your God onto others
What is to be done?

See the world as a beautiful vase
made out of clay
It is fascinating and complex

You want to know how the vase is made
You dig into the clay
and tear it apart looking for the answer
Only to be left with a pile of clay
and the vase is no longer

Realizing what you are looking for
cannot be found in the form of the vase
It is in the vibration of what created the vase

The world functions similarly
You cannot fix the form of injustice
It is not in the form
It is in the vibration of what created the injustice

Morality is a product of the outer world
The same place where injustice lives
Stemming from the vibration of beliefs and thoughts

For lasting change to occur in the world
transformation is required
by being in alignment with Eternal Source
Therefore
all actions will be moved
by and through the vibration of love

This is what changes the world

Driving down a busy road
People rushing to beat the traffic lights
Thinking:
Look at all these people
all in a rush going nowhere fast
Music playing from the radio
Dancing in my car seat
while waiting at the red light

A woman drives up next to me
in a convertible sports car
Also
dancing to the music on her radio
Our eyes meet briefly
We both start
laughing and dancing
crazier and harder

Our connection is familiar
even though I never met her
and probably will never see her again
But on some level
we know each other
The level of Heart and joy

The light changes green and I wave to her
and she waves back with a big smile
The motion of love and joy fills my being
Thinking:
This is the kind of world I want to live in

⚬⚬

Life
Wrapped in a bubble of illusion

Temporary
Short-lived
and transient

Can pop at any moment

How can life be taken so seriously
when passing by so swiftly?

But then again
how can it not?

⚬

A SACRED MOMENT:
BE THE WORLD YOU WANT TO LIVE IN

One of the greatest insights unfolding through the wisdom and knowledge of science and spirituality is the awareness that the world is not a separate entity. It is an extension of frequency, energy, and vibration from thoughts, beliefs, feelings, and inspired action. It is an extension of the collective consciousness of humanity, as well as each individual person. All too often, we place the focus on what is *not wanted* in our world of experience, instead of what *is wanted* or desired. By raising the collective consciousness, human society can create a thriving and loving world—it is in our hands.

The illusion and magic of life, which some call *maya*, is believing the world we sense is permanent, unchanging, and outside of ourselves. In actuality, the outside world is a mirror of the expressions and reflections of who we are: it is then experienced and interpreted within our inner self or inner world.

The world's reflection is similar to looking at yourself in a mirror. If you want to see how a hat looks on you, you do not put the hat on the reflection and expect it to be on you. For the mirror to reflect yourself wearing the hat, you *must first put the hat on you*, and then the mirror will reflect you wearing it. Whether you like the hat or not is your decision. Same with the world—put on the hat you prefer to wear and the mirrors of the world will reflect the image. *Be what you want to experience: then your experience will Be.*

You cannot change every person in the world. However, you can change yourself and your world, which creates the momentum of energy expanding to family and community, as well as globally and universally, a momentum affecting every particle of existence. If you want change, Be the world you want to live in.

CONTEMPLATION

Close your eyes, inhale and exhale deeply for three cycles or more. When you feel settled and centered, ask yourself the question:

What kind of world do I want to live in?

Will it be a world of love, happiness, peace, joyfulness, caring, kindness, tolerance, compassion, inspiration, support, abundance, respect, community, prosperity, health, sharing, and consciousness?

Will it be a world of cooperation with all life-forms cohabiting our Earth: humans, animals, plants, trees, and insects living in a loving, peaceful coexistence?

Next, contemplate, eyes still closed, how you can bring the world you desire into your personal life. What actions can you take? For instance, saying kind and loving words to your children, partners, and friends; being helpful and friendly with your neighbors and smiling at people in the supermarket or slowing down at a merging traffic area to allow a car to proceed in your lane; supporting your local animal or homeless shelters by donating time or money; respecting the Earth by choosing environmentally friendly products and actions. And most importantly, caring for your body, mind, and spirit for health and prosperity.

Once you have a few thoughts and ideas on how you can support the kind of world you want to live in, inhale and exhale deeply, then breathe normally. Focus on the inhalation and exhalation of your breath and sit in silence for a minute or two.

JOURNAL

Slowly open your eyes. Take a few moments and jot down the thoughts and ideas you received during the contemplation and how you can integrate them into your daily life.

You can do this practice daily or as often as you wish: clarity and direction will surface. Go out into the world wearing the hat you desire, and *Be the world you want to live in.*

2

THOUGHTS BEFORE MATTER

Matter is hardened thoughts

Do not sleep any longer
Wake up

You are addicted to thoughts of slumber
and complain you cannot open your eyes
An excuse to continue sleeping

Wake up!

What needs to be open
is the Eye of Heart
The center highway where
thoughts and matter mingle

A realized Soul
feels and acts from Heart
Heart lets mind know of its importance
Heart lets mind know when it is off track
Heart lets mind know
thoughts before matter

Wake up!

Know your story
Know thoughts and beliefs
create and sustain it
The Inner World is where your story's image begins
to form
The outer world is where you experience your story
in form

Wake up!

There are two main worlds:
Consciousness and unconsciousness

The world of Consciousness
is one of depth
The world of unconsciousness
is one of shallowness

The world of Consciousness
creates deliberately
The world of unconsciousness
creates carelessly

Consciousness leads to infinite subtle mystical worlds
Unconsciousness leads to a brick wall

Everything in the manifested world
comes from humanity

Originating from the vibration of thought
Birthing out of love or fear

The Great Revolution
the community of humans are now facing
is our Face

The Face of what we are presenting to the world

No more hiding heads in the sand
No more blaming

Look at your open hands

Fill them by
assuming the Responsibility
of the world we all share

❦

DIVINE OBSERVATION ON KARMA

A man talking to his colleague during lunch:

"My parents told me that my grandparents had it. The whole family was warned about it being passed down to their children. And I should be on the lookout for it all the time."

"Wow! What are doing about it?" asked the colleague.

"I have to prepare for when it comes. I go to the doctor and check my body for it all the time. The doctor takes a bunch of tests on a regular basis, so it could be detected early and cut it out before it grows."

The colleague shook his head and said, "Bad karma I guess."

The man agreed.

WISDOM SPEAKS

Karma is not being helpless from the momentum of past actions
generations or lifetimes
Karma is when you choose to allow the past to come into the Now
Generating a past entity of thought and belief systems

The disease is not passed down
The thoughts and beliefs
that created the disease are passed down

If you stand on karma believing it is an unchangeable destiny
the low-vibration entity becomes a heavy brick of helplessness
Power diminishes
If you stand on karma knowing belief patterns are changeable
the high-vibration entity becomes a springboard to freedom
Power magnifies

CG

You cannot pluck
a problem out and toss it aside
It will find its way back

You cannot get rid
of a problem by putting a lid on it
It will explode and manifest into unpleasantness

Problems are in the river of thoughts and beliefs
They are not things
They are streams of energy

Can you pluck a piece of water out of the river
and expect the river to be different?
No

However
you can redirect the river
You can redirect the energy of thoughts and beliefs

Then the river flows in a new direction
Then the thoughts and beliefs flow in a new direction

The old dries up and nothing is left behind

Knowing how far you can go
you first have to acknowledge the destination is near
Thoughts are *individual moment frames*
No movement
No time
All within the present

The illusion of movement and time
are thoughts remembering and imagining

Thoughts are little bundles of *energetic-vibrations* called sound
formed by the Light of Mind

*Thoughts are faster than the speed of light
projecting Life's Living Picture*

The nature of thought is magnetic
Attracting what the thought is thinking
Sticking like flypaper
Creating the frames for your Life's movie

Consciousness gives personal mind the awareness of itself
Enabling you to see the premier

Life's experiences are snapshots
of here and now
Disguised in thoughts of
there and later

There is a contrast between *every thing* and *Everything*
The misunderstanding is
within the subtle distinguishing

The complexity of the world focuses on *every thing*
Separateness
The simplicity of Existence encompasses *Everything*
Inclusive

The wise do not know *every thing*
Impossible to achieve

But they are intimately connected
to the Essence of what *Everything* is
And are able
to process the Knowledge and Insight
of *Everything*
behind *every thing*

SACRED REFLECTION

Who is thinking my thoughts?

Observe the thinker of your thoughts

The thinker is affectionately linked to both:
The conditioned being
your humanness
And the unconditioned Being
your Spirit

When the link is stronger to the conditioned being
the power is misplaced
And the thinker has a mind of its own

When the link is stronger to the unconditioned Being
The power lies in the Higher Perspective
And the thinker listens to Guidance

Lovingly
both are always heard

Who is thinking your thoughts depends
on the link to whom you are giving the power

⌒⊂⊃

The Origin of Creation
stems from the insight of Perception
giving birth to the many worlds

Be conscious of this

Layer upon layer
And within the layers
are more layers

It is amazing

Look into the essence of life
An endless universe
Physical
Mental
Emotional
Spiritual
Etheric
Energy
Vibration
Infinite dimensions

Perception infiltrates them all
creating the Space
where the real and unreal kiss
to seal the precise moment of Creation

꧁꧂

We all want to be free of mind's grasp

We already are free of its hold
But we are enslaved by the strong pull
of judgments

Preferences will always exist
At times
carrying the heavy load of judgments on their back
leaving no room to breath
Measuring what is right or wrong
Preaching there is only one way to worship
Rules and regulations for whom to love
Stating facts and absolutes about life

The trap is believing the judgments are real
Judgments are just perceptions of your beliefs
An opinion
They have no solidity of their own
Living in the realm of fantasy

Personal preference is what feels good or not
The illusion of judgment springs from preference

Enjoy your preferences
they bring vivid color and depth to your life's surroundings
However
when your preferences are placed on others as judgments
wearing the false cloak of truth
the color is sucked out
And the landscape becomes flat and gray

Thoughts harden like rocks
from the sediment of feelings and beliefs
Buried deep
Compacted and cemented together
by individual and collective programmed consciousness

A consciousness that is *before*
during and *after* this lifetime
Manifesting form in the projected and shared world
Mistakenly taken as real and unchanging

The programmed consciousness
is represented in each individual
And forms neurological networks
of beliefs about reality
called *samskaras*

The individual interpretation of these beliefs
is the making of you
Samskaras are the joining of neuron networks
locking together to make up the grid of you
Thus
blindly following the grid like a robot

The ancient languages have many words
for the Inner Kingdoms
However
not so much for the outer world

The modern languages have many words
for the outer world
However
not so much for the inner kingdoms

Complete liberation or *moksha* is to be free
of the hold of samskaras

First by distinguishing the human
as a conditioned being
And realizing the route of beliefs and thoughts
can be changed to a
more liberating existence

One can remain asleep or be awake in life

When sleeping
the samskaras or neuron networks
take hold of your reality by
repeating the same avenues of beliefs and thoughts
Creating the same scenarios in your physicality
Wanted or not

When Awake
the avenues are known
And you have a choice to stay on the same route
or take the next exit to create another avenue

Surrender to *what is*

Especially when
the momentum of an unwanted belief
is gaining strength by flexing its muscle
in the manifested world

Change is close
But it is not in the world

Surrender does not mean giving up
Quite the contrary
Surrender means letting go
And
allowing the dust of thoughts to settle
with no interference

When letting go
the *origin of circumstance* and how it operates
will be seen

Once seen
expansion occurs
and the directives are from your
Greater Self not your lesser self

Resistance ceases
Cooperation increases
Now
change has a chance
to change

Life is cyclical
Know the difference between the
conscious rhythms of Cycles
and the unconscious habitual cycles

Take notice
All of life is cyclical:
Sunrise and sunset
Seasons and moon phases
Waves of the ocean
Inhalation and exhalation of breath
Beat of heart
Life and death

Alignment with nature's rhythms of Cycles
can carry you
Alignment with habitual cycles of addictive thoughts
will stunt you

Habits block
Rhythms allow
Distinguish the difference

Within habits
nothing can grow
The soil is depleted from overuse
Within rhythms
everything grows
Replenishing at every new cycle

Rhythm is the pulse of life
Find your Rhythm and ride with all of existence

When thoughts fill your mind
leaving no space for Awareness to enter
it is called a disturbed state of mind

When Awareness fills the mind
leaving no space for thoughts to enter
it is called a peaceful state of mind

A SACRED MOMENT:
THOUGHTS BEFORE MATTER

Being aware and mindful that everything in the manifested world originates from a spark of thought, presents insight into the process of creation. The invention of chairs, pencils, automobiles, houses, art, music, careers and even babies, along with the experiences of events and circumstances, all begin with a thought. When thoughts develop into feelings, beliefs, dreams, desires, or goals, the energy intensifies because it *matters*. In other words, everything you experience originates from the *vibrational-frequency* of thought. Thoughts are power houses when focused and directed. And the vibration of thought is sound. This is the secret the ancient ones spoke of.

We were taught in school that the physical world is made up of matter. Matter is mostly a solid, liquid, or gas. It is called matter because it *matters*: important and significant. Matter enables us to explore, sense, and experience the external world— the joyful aspect of life. However, if you break down matter to its simplest unit, it is an atom. An atom is mostly made of space, energy, vibration, and frequency. Therefore, the external world, the world we sense, operates in the energy-field of vibration and frequency— the Unified Field of the residence where all matter lives.

When something is important, the *vibrational-frequency* of thoughts, beliefs, and feelings create a frequency that becomes the *attracting catalyst* for other similar frequencies; then starts forming or manifesting of *what matters to you,* in the physical world. Focus, excitement, and passion add to the attracting frequencies. And what matters, what is important to you, seeks you, instead of you seeking it.

See yourself as a tuning fork. A tuning fork is a metal two-pronged acoustic resonator and when hit with a rubber mallet emits a certain frequency or tone. If you set up two tuning forks of the same tone, a few inches apart, and hit one of the forks, it will cause the other fork to resonate to the same frequency. Comparatively, if you set two tuning forks of different tones and hit one, the other fork will not vibrate or resonate.

As a human tuning fork, you set the tone of who you are, through your thoughts, beliefs, feelings, attitudes, and actions, which attracts "like" tones and frequencies of the world into your circumstances. Like attracts like. You can be conscious of this phenomenon or not. However, it always follows this principle: You set the tone of who you are, and who you are sets the tone of your experience.

CONTEMPLATION

Close your eyes, inhale and exhale deeply for three cycles or more. When you feel settled and centered, ask yourself the question:

What thoughts are creating my circumstances?

Are your thoughts focused on lack or more? Love or fear? Tolerance or judgement? Happiness or sadness? Health or sickness? Confidence or doubt? Acceptance or rejection? Anger or contentment? What occupies your mind?

Next, contemplate, eyes still closed, what circumstance in your life you would like to change. Be mindful of the thoughts that are creating the attraction for this experience. If you lack money, what thoughts are you thinking: "I never have enough money; the rich are taking all the money away from the common folk." If you have health issues, your thoughts may be: "My mother had it and it is just a matter of time until I will get it; I will always have this disease, it is not curable," and so on. These are the catalysts of thoughts creating the continuation of the unwanted circumstance.

Once you have a few thoughts and ideas on what is creating your unwanted circumstance, inhale and exhale deeply, then breathe normally. Focus on the inhalation and exhalation of your breath and sit in silence for a minute or two.

JOURNAL

Slowly open your eyes. Take a few minutes and jot down the thoughts and ideas surrounding the circumstance you would like to change. Write down all the thoughts you have concerning this circumstance. Just being aware of the *thought-circumstance connection* will bring change.

Allow the habit of unwanted expectations to be different. Next to the unwanted thought, write the wanted thought to replace it. Stay simple, general, and make sure it feels good. For example:

"The rich have all the money." *Replace* it with, "Money is abundant and there is enough money for everyone."

"I never have enough money." *Replace* it with, "I will allow more in my life."

"My parents had a disease and I will have it." *Replace* it with, "I am not my parents and can create a different health experience."

"I will always have this disease." *Replace* it with, "Well-being is predominant in my body."

"I will never have a loving relationship with another person." *Replace* it with, "The loving relationship I desire is with myself first."

You can do this practice daily or as often as you wish with other circumstances that you would like to change or shift: clarity and direction will surface. Go out into the world with the knowledge close to your heart—*thoughts before matter.*

3

DANCE YOUR DANCE

You are the only one who hears the music for your Dance

Learn the art of harmony
One never has to compromise the tone
of their true feelings

If you play too many chords to appease others
it is difficult to hear your song

The art of harmony plays your music
attracting the tones and chords
of those who want to dance with you

To stay in harmony
is to stay true to yourself
by loving yourself
Dancing your Dance

Observe nature:
You do not see a daisy forcing
a rose to be like itself
They grow together in harmony
and dance in the wind

And the beauty of both is appreciated

The trees and flowers move to
the *rhythm's pull* of sunlight
The clouds slide across the dance floor of the sky
The heart beats
The breath moves

All aware of the musical Composition
and the part they play

Your music is contained in Soul
It is always singing the tune softly into your ear
And heart creates the beat

Listen

When you turn to it
Soul smiles
When you do not turn to it
Soul smiles

When you Dance to it
Soul is ecstatic

Each heartbeat sends a message

A universal message
unique for each individual

Feel the pulse Life offers:
In and out
On and off
One moment you are here
and the next you are not

Pulling you closer to Center

The beat is to know
you exist

The message is to know
it is only for a short time

Within your breath
lies all the answers and solutions
Within your breath
lies the completeness in incompleteness
Within your breath
lies the simplicity in complexity

The breath represents the rising and falling of
the manifested world
The Rising of Expansion comes from *That*
And the Returning of Surrender goes back into *That*
Observe:
The movement of the ocean's waves
Flowers bloom and return to Earth
Sunrise and sunset
Waking up and retiring to sleep
Standing up and sitting down
Birth and death

Life's participants follow the music
from the desire to grow and Expand
and eventually surrender and Return
The breath is a constant reminder

What allows Expansiveness is Surrender
Life is riding the waves
and living in *That*
which All comes From and falls back Into

Twirl like the Sufis
Dance in the funnel
where only the One exists

The seed of the daisy is planted in the ground
Watch as it grows

It is not becoming something other than a daisy
It is becoming what it *already is*
The blueprint within the seed

Humans follow the same Law

The dilemma is when you allow thoughts and beliefs to attach
to other than what your seed contains
Thus
stifling your Authentic Self to surface

Wandering through life without meaning
Always feeling something is missing

Not listening to Soul
is the missing part in the equation
of you being You

SACRED REFLECTION

How do I hear the music to dance my Dance?

In the wind
the daisies sway differently
than the roses

Each dancing to the tone of their Beingness

Your tone is sung by Soul
in the form of your passions
Listen

Then dance to the beat of Heart

಑

If you dance to the same unpleasant music
over and over again
you will get the same results
over and over again
Trapped within the walls of limitation

The grooves grow deep within the dance floor
from the repeated steps
So deep
eventually it becomes difficult to move
The dance is no longer
Stuck in one place
Continuing to listen
to the binding and suffocating music

Dance your Dance in the dark first
by facing what you must
And look up and listen to the new music
from the heavens within

The dark allows the sparks
of your steps to be seen
Igniting the flame of your new Dance

You may have to bounce against the walls
from the grooves you created

But eventually
the grooves will mysteriously disappear

❧

Pay attention to the space between
things and events
Focusing only on things and events
one could get lost

Pay attention to the space between
thoughts and feelings
Focusing only on thoughts and feelings
one could get lost

Music is heard
because of the space between the notes

The world could only be known
from the space between things and events
The mind and body could only be known
from the space between thoughts and feelings
Space is always present
delivering a more expansive view

If you were walking in nature
and only focused on the color green
all the colors of the rainbow
the Earth offers
would be missed

If you only focused on things and events
All That Is would be missed
Dance in the space
Soul offers to Spirit
The merging of Soul and Spirit is your Residence
housing who you truly are

DIVINE OBSERVATION ON LISTENING TO SOUL

A young man would secretly dance in the barn at night when no one was watching, other than the horses and goats. In the dim light he would imagine being on stage and flying in the air to the most beautiful music.

One day at a dance recital, the young man was working with his brother adjusting and repairing the light fixtures on the stage. He was watching the rehearsal of the dancers. He could not take his eyes off them. He had a smile on his face from ear to ear. He was totally absorbed and felt he did not have a body... just air.

His brother called his name and then poked him. "What is the matter with you? I was calling your name and you didn't answer? Are you deaf?"

The young man dropped his head in shame, afraid of revealing his passion. He mustered up enough courage and said, "I want to see the whole performance."

"We have work to do," his brother barked. "Get your ass moving."

As they walked out of the theater, the young man kept turning around to look at the stage. He bumped into an older man who almost fell to the floor. "Oh, I am sorry," apologized the young man.

The older man laughed and said, "You must love dance, I see it in your eyes and your body seems limber and loose. Here, please take my card, I am a director of a dance studio, come and visit."

The young man looked at the card and then looked up at the man and smiled. He put the card in his shirt pocket, the pocket closest to his heart.

"Maybe one day," he whispered to himself.

WISDOM SPEAKS

The only day is Now
The only time is Now

There are two kinds of hearing:
One from the outer world
One from the Inner World

But there is only one kind of Listening:
Soul speaking and guiding
to expose your Authentic Self

You will never know the joy of a fulfilling life
if you do not Listen

We are individual flames
Some brighter than others
Some fan the flame and others smother it

Watch a candle's flame

It burns bright with stillness

When it extinguishes
the smoke lingers
Dancing spirally to the heavens
Eventually disappearing

The flame and you
share an intimate short journey

Will you fan your flame or smother it?

You are a creator
This is your birthright

You are a mapmaker
This is your talent

You choose your thoughts
This is your power

You manifest from feelings
This is your way

You enjoy
This is your inheritance

Accept this and reveal the secret
of the beauty of your humanness

⌒⌒

The Sacred Matrix of life is composed of
luminous *energy-vibration* avenues

Avenues connecting all aspects of existence:
From the stone to the mountain
From the insect to the plant
From the beast to the human
From the atom to the universe

Interacting and dancing with each other
forming the grid of Divine Design

The tree's matrix dances with the
sun and water
earth and nature
to find the avenues of tones
to create harmony
in its surroundings

The human matrix hovers
outside the body and extends to the infinite

Following instructions from thoughts and beliefs
orchestrated by feelings
Creating the grid and blueprint for the Dance of life

Love and joy are pleasing arrangements
A melody All recognize
and dance in synchronicity

If sidetracked by out of tune interruptions
of fear and discord
the dance is not flowing
And it is out of step with the rest of the dance troupe

The avenues of the Sacred Matrix
are the highways connecting All to All
affecting All and All

Happiness and love create a symphony
for All to Dance in harmony

Even a fly that lands on your arm
will recognize the melody

Dancing
then you go Back

Singing
then you go Back

Playing
then you go Back

Awake
Get to know the part you go Back to
The part which remains constant and is in between activity

By going Back
you will know how to move forward

⌒◎⌒

The atoms dance in harmony
to the music from your focused attention

Creating a composition
of your desire
to be manifested and experienced

A SACRED MOMENT:
DANCING YOUR DANCE

Living a full life is listening to the music of your Soul and dancing your Dance. Your Dance is being your Authentic Self and presenting it on the world's stage—a life with excitement, joy, and wonder. Your Dance is the swaying and moving to the beat of your Heart, directed from your Soul's passions. Your passions govern the steps of your desires. Your Dance, your expression, is unique and adds to the repertoire of life's composition. If your Dance remains hidden, you deny the world of your full potential.

If you are admiring an oil painting of a beautiful nature scene from a distance, the mountains, rivers, flowers, sky, clouds, and meadows are distinct and become your main focus. As you walk closer to the painting, the strokes from the paint brush become more evident, taking your focus away from the whole scene to each individual brush strokes of color. Each stroke creates the whole picture in the painting. One misplaced stroke or absent stroke affects and changes the whole painting. Similarly, all life forms, including you, are the individual strokes of light and color adding to the World's Life Picture.

If the flowers did not bloom and the trees did not reach for the sun, if the chickens did not hatch and the sun stayed hidden behind the clouds, and if the infant remained in the womb and the stars did not shine—the world would not Be. And know, the blooming of your existence, your Dance, is an integral aspect of the creation of the world.

The force of existence is the force behind the Becoming. We are meant to bloom: honesty and courage must prevail. Listen to your passions, excitements, and desires. Dance to the rhythm of who you are—your Authentic Self. Bless the world with your Dance and Light, for your beauty is creating Life's Living Picture.

CONTEMPLATION

Close your eyes, inhale and exhale deeply for three cycles or more. When you feel settled and centered, ask yourself the question:

What are my passions in life and am I living them?

Are you following your true desires? Are you listening to your Heart? Are you doing what you love and feeling excited about it? Are you following your bliss? Are you paying attention to the music from the passions of your Soul?

Next, contemplate, eyes still closed, what your desires and passions truly are, what brings excitement to you. They may be hidden deep within, covered over with fears, procrastination, and insecurity. They may even have been forgotten. But let me assure you, they are present. You may have to dig deep. But they will surface with a little focus, exploration, and a desire to know. For instance, your passions may be singing, painting, working with animals or children, dancing, gardening, writing, being an entrepreneur, having a love or soul partner, spirituality, or politics. The list is endless.

Once you have a few thoughts and ideas, inhale and exhale deeply, then breathe normally. Focus on the inhalation and exhalation of your breath and sit in silence for a minute or two.

JOURNAL

Slowly open your eyes. Take a few minutes and jot down two or three of your desires and passions. If you are not sure yet, write down some possibilities or ideas about how you can start exploring and researching. Next to the desire, write a few things you can do today that will support your passion: explore classes or read about people who are doing what you want, research, read books, or take a workshop.

You can do this practice daily or as often as you wish: clarity and direction will surface. Go out into the world with the image close to your Heart and *dance your Dance,* starting today!

4

BE TRUE TO TRUTH

When truth is spoken
it cuts like a knife
Truth speaks truth
no matter what is being said

Within the world
exists *true* and *not true*
Then there is Truth

The Truth about what is true and not true
is that the world offers them simultaneously
Keen discernment is necessary to distinguish them

It is true we need money to live
It is not true living depends on money

It is true we are alive
It is not true we are all living

It is true that physical beauty is beautiful
It is not true that beauty is physical

It is true material things can be fulfilling
It is not true that material things can fulfill you

It is true birth and death are inevitable for the body
It is not true they affect the Eternal You

The essence of Truth is the home of true and not true

To know what is true is to know Truth
To know what is not true is to know Truth

It lies within
To look elsewhere is fruitless
It is everywhere and nowhere
Once you find Truth
The world will be true to you

No longer will you be fooled by false images
It is no longer in you

Far from the world
yet
smack in the middle

To know universal Truth
know your individual truth
It requires intimacy

Look at the world as yourself
See the opposites:
Ugly and beautiful
Strong and weak
Young and old
Love and fear
You are both and neither
What connects them?
Truth

Gaze into another's eyes
Separateness dissolves

The Truth you are seeking is
You are an Eternal Being
All comes from you and eagerly awaits its return

What is beyond Truth?
Love
This is the Truth about truth

෴

Raise the level of expectation
Trust Eternal Source

It knows where to bring you

It is here already
waiting patiently with open arms for your arrival

⁓

If your truth is causing discomfort
ask the question:
is it the Ultimate Truth or
is it just true your beliefs are causing the pain?

Your truth is established by how much you believe it is true

Your truths are not entities with their own breath

The force behind them is the intensity of belief
No matter what it is

Your reality
including your truths
are agreements with your
personal self and society
history and mass consciousness

Choice maintains them or not
Once an agreement is changed
your truth no longer exists

This is the Ultimate Truth

The moon has cycles
Circling the Earth
Catching a ride around the sun

Rising over the horizon and reaching the heights
to illuminate the darkest of dark nights

The mystery of the moon has been the subject
of wonder for eons

The full moon
sheds light
And allows life in the dark

The new moon
Shows the beauty of the dark
And allows the light of every star to be seen

Both occasions
create the excitement of uncovering the essence of Light
In the dark or the light

The moon mirrors the revelation
of its direct connection to you

The design of the tide of emotions
expressing Light

⟳

SACRED REFLECTION

What is the Ultimate Truth?

The Ultimate Truth is the truth you believe is true
Nothing more and nothing less

◦◦◦

THE BELLY OF LIBERATION

Truth is both liberating and agonizing. There is no denying the fear, pain, sadness, and anger that exist in your world are very unpleasant. However, the constant focus on unpleasantness somehow serves you. It is a distraction and a self-worth issue. It is more painful to face your Face than to experience the unpleasant pain.

You contain the image of the greatest creative force. Every encounter is an encounter with your Greater Self, which is beyond the falsehood realms of thought. You are a Divine Lover— open your eyes and Heart. You must begin to love yourself before you can receive the message:

Your personal self is wrapped with the love of GodSelf
This is where freedom lies
Be courageous and admit it
No judging
No blaming

Just admit it
to no one but yourself

Face your true Face

Be vulnerable in this disclosure
It gives room for the agony to flip over
and bare the belly of liberation

Come to Me
And stay with Me

Bring Me all your doings
Invite Me to all your celebrations
Allow Me to carry you through your storms

Within every breath
my Breath speaks
Within every beat of heart
my Heart loves

Listen
Feel

Come to Me
It only takes focus and surrender
to lighten the heavy thoughts of illusion

The game of existence is to find Me again
But you really never left

Surprise

⌒☙⌒

We are bundles of Light
infused with divine information and knowledge

Stars speak of origin
Dark speaks of exposure
Space speaks of our infiniteness
and the order of life speaks of love

Love the Light that directs you
Allow it to reveal the Love that is
You

Hearing the words of Truth
sets a motion in the body
The whole body responds by saying
Yes
Not to the words
Yes
to Truth
For words cannot be truth
Two people can hear the same words
one will hear an utterance and one will hear Truth

Where is Truth to be found?
It is found where Love and Truth dance together as One
In the state of Truth
Love is present
In the state of Love
Truth is present
For instance
words from a lover are words of love expressing Truth

The Truth of anything or anyone always stems from Love

Love is not in the words
but from the feelings the words project
If love is felt
Truth is felt
No matter what words are spoken

One doesn't have to say
I love you to express love
All one has to do is love
and all words will be words of Love

When face-to-face with another
you are face-to-face with yourself
Acknowledging Oneness

When looking at another
do not get lost in their face and think
it is *my* face looking at *their* face
Justifying separateness

Can you see your face without a mirror?
It cannot be done
The manifested world mirrors whatever holds your attention

To see the other as You
is wisdom

To see the other to justify you
is ignorance

Justification
is taking truth to its falsehood
Proving your separateness
Continuing the cycle of unconsciousness
with fear fueling the motion

When you see the other as You
you are taking Truth to it highest realm
Bathing in pure consciousness
with love fueling the depths of Being

This is your Home
The Sacred Residence of Absorption

All religions and spiritual teachings speak of truth
However
Truth is a paradox
Discrimination is a must

The truth of a Christian
is different from the truth of a Muslim
The truth of a Yogi
is different from the truth of a Buddhist
The truth of an atheist
is different from the truth of a theist
And so on

If truth is claimed to be in the words spoken
it is not Truth at all
Absolute Truth is beyond words and dogma
Truth cannot live on the waves of language
thoughts and concepts
for its residence is in the deepest of oceans

It is all-inclusive
Intertwined within the nature of existence

The Truth
we are all seeking to experience
is to drink from its Cup
Once tasted
it could never be spoken

*If you drink a cup of sweet fruit juice
can another taste it from your words of description?*

SACRED OBSERVATION ON TRUTH

"There is a robbery at the bakery!" screamed a customer. "Call the police, quick!"

The police came and asked what happened.

"That woman stole bread!" yelled a man in an agitated and angry voice. And all the people pointed to the same woman. She looked tired and dusty, her hair pushed up into a white cap, and she wore slippers for shoes.

She tried to speak, but the police officer said, "Quiet, woman!" He would not even allow the saleswoman behind the counter to speak. There was too much confusion, and people in the bakery were in an uproar.

The police officer gathered the people and asked again, "What happened?"

One patron said, "I saw the whole thing. She," pointing to the dusty woman, "came in, walked up to the counter, and blatantly stole the bread and left. I could not believe my eyes."

Another patron said, "I saw her by the counter. She distracted the saleswoman by asking her a question. When the saleswoman turned around, she reached over and took the bread."

Still another patron said, "I heard her say something about being hungry and begging for bread ... and the salesperson handed her a loaf of bread."

"Arrest her!" people in the bakery barked.

"I am sick of these homeless people taking advantage and sponging off everyone," said an enraged woman.

Meanwhile, children outside the bakery looked into the large store window and watched the angry crowd with worried eyes.

The crowd became rowdy, chanting, "Arrest her! Arrest her!"

The police officer put handcuffs on the dusty woman and

said to the crowd, "I want the truth. Did she steal the bread, distract the salesperson and reach over the counter to take the bread, or did she beg for the bread by saying she was hungry? I want the truth!" said the police officer in a commanding voice.

"Please let me speak," said the woman. "It is all true. I came in and took the bread, I reached over the counter to take the bread, and I did say something about being hungry."

"Okay, that settles it. You are going to the precinct."

"Please wait! You are missing the underlying truth," said the dusty woman.

"Oh yeah, what's that?" the officer asked sarcastically.

"I own the store! I did reach over and take the bread while my worker went into the back of the store to get more food to feed the children in the alley. They are hungry." The woman pointed to the disheveled children outside the window.

Silence came over the store as the people noticed the scared children looking through the window, witnessing the fiasco.

"Why do you look so dusty and tired?" asked one woman.

"I am tired because I was baking all night for the holidays. I am covered in flour, not dust."

The people put their heads down in shame. A stillness and silence overcame the bakery.

The store owner broke the silence and said, "Buy something for the children to eat. Let their perception of you be one of love and not hate."

Everyone lined up, including the police officer and bought donuts, bread, rolls, and cookies for the children and their families.

The storeowner's heart swelled with love. She smiled and said, "I better start baking, we will run out of everything soon. This is my best day ever!"

WISDOM SPEAKS

Please do not be so quick to judge
Truth has many faces which are never really true anyway

Be aware that truth is only a perception within the moment
The moment only
However
in the state of Love
the residence of Truth always lives

Close your eyes
Focus on a point of concentration within your mindscape
This is how the endless flow of meditation begins

It opens the door to the infinite
and takes you on a ride of fluidity

A roller coaster ride reaching the top
to savor the Above View
quiet and still
timeless and aware
Joining
place to place
people to people

Nothing more to know
Nothing more to do

The vastness of nothingness and everythingness
merges within the Vision of Being

A place
where Sight is Seen
with eyes opened or closed

⌒

The circle of Truth
orbits the Center

The Center holds the nature of Truth
Love

To know Truth
one must listen

To listen
one must be still

To be still
is the nature of Truth

A SACRED MOMENT:
TRUTH

Truth is intertwined with belief: making the rope of existence where one cannot live without the other. The truths of one religion are based on its beliefs. However, it could be quite different from the truths and beliefs of another religion. Which one holds the Truth?

A person who believes that life is a struggle and unfair will continue to experience that truth. Another's belief that life is an adventure and fun will continue to experience that truth. Which one holds the Truth?

The sad part is, there is no real truth. The happy part is that it is in your hands. Belief and interpretation have dominance over truth, therefore, subject to change. The changeable truth has nothing to do with the Eternal or Ultimate Truth you are seeking. The Eternal Truth of who you are: changeless, loving, nonjudgmental, and eternal.

There is a part of you that remains changeless through all the changes of your existence: You were a baby, then an adolescent and now, an adult. You went through many changes in your life. We can all agree that as an adult, your body, thoughts, attitudes, and feelings are very different from when you were a baby. Yet, there is a You that remains changeless through all the changes. A You observing and witnessing your life's experiences. A You observing you.

The truth you are seeking lies within, beyond your senses, thoughts, and beliefs, exposing the aspect of You, your True Self. A You that is aware of Awareness and conscious of Consciousness, looking *through* your eyes, not *from* your eyes—revealing the Eternal Truth: You are Eternal.

CONTEMPLATION

Close your eyes, inhale and exhale slowly for three cycles or more. When you feel settled and centered, ask yourself the question:

What is my Truth?

Are you human or spirit or both? Are you finite or infinite or both? Is life temporary or eternal or both? Is your nature immortal or mortal or both? Is life real or illusionary or both? Is your truth filled with love or fear or both?

Next, contemplate, eyes still closed, how you can live your Eternal Truth in your daily life. Focusing on the part of you that has been with you through all the changes of your life. The Eternal Truth is the Eternal Self encompassing *All is Well*. By being happy, peaceful, loving, wise, grateful, insightful, and joyful, as well as knowing your physical life is temporary and appreciating every moment, is how you live your Eternal Truth. You then extend your actions toward all living beings using the attitudes of tolerance, integrity, understanding, love, kindness, and compassion. To live your Eternal Truth is to identify with your Greater Perspective: the changeless Eternal Self.

Once you have a few thoughts and ideas, inhale and exhale deeply, then breathe normally. Focus on the inhalation and exhalation of your breath and sit in silence for a minute or two.

JOURNAL

Slowly open eyes. Take a few minutes and jot down three aspects of how you can incorporate your Eternal Truth into your day. If you pick the aspect of being loving, jot down how you can be loving during daily activities. Loving to friends, family, animals, plants and most importantly, being loving to yourself.

You can do this practice daily or as often as you wish: clarity and direction will surface. And live the day with the Eternal Truth as your guide allowing the unveiling of the *Truth about truth*.

5

THE FUTURE IS NOW

In the flux of time
the past
present and future
dissolve in the Now

The only place to Be
is Now

Within the Present
the past and future are tricks of the mind

The memories of the past
are remembered Now
The dreams of the future
are imagined Now

Being present
is where Presence lives
The Omnipresence
with no constrictions of time
with no constrictions of locality

The past is coming from
The future is moving to

Both fusing together
in the fleeting moment of the Now
where neither can be found

⌒⚮⌒

The idea of the future is cradled by Soul

Soul knows your hero and heroine's journey on this earth
When you embrace it
the path will light up

Imagination is key
Feelings are your guide
Joy is the result

Taking the first step on the Lighted Path
requires courage
Facing the demons of falsehoods
believed to be real

Be an illustrious warrior

Hold the sword of enlightenment
and walk the future's path
Now

Isn't it funny how the old ways
are now the new ways

To be natural
and conscious of the Earth's ways are in trend

To plant gardens and eat whole foods
To meditate and move the body
Both appear to be something new for health and well-being

However
The new ways are nothing new

Looking closely
the old ways were always standing by
Whispering the natural ways of the wise
with the guidance of the body's knowledge

The closer we look
the more it will be revealed
that the old ways are not old at all

We just forgot how to listen

The mind is your best ally
It is where your *personal perspective*
is able to recognize your *Expansive Perspective*

It rests on a pivot point and could be swayed
by the winds of thinking
Thinking is an activity in the realm of time

When the mind is in the Now
space opens for Divine thought

Thought is a gift from the higher realms
wrapped in an idea
It is dropped into the space provided
to inspire with insight
in the Field of Love

Divine thought is in the realm of *All That Is*
It is not an activity until you start thinking about it
Mind unites your personal and expansive selves
or disbands them

The mind seems to have a mind of its own
when you allow it
Always in forward or backwards motion
Always in the past or future
In worry or control
In fear or misery

The mind can set you free
or
keep you imprisoned

To feel Presence
one has to be present and mindful

You search and search for divine guidance
Seeking to touch the Light

The searching suggests it is something outside of yourself

Communication is only within Presence
A vortex devoid of past and future
Just Now

Meditation and prayer
wrapped in silence and sincerity
are the communication lines to GodSelf

This is the time to ask your deepest questions
Your answers will be given

Your direct line is with you always
Calling you to be present within Presence

Self-worth is a misunderstood phrase

A connotation of putting worth on self or value on self
Value is an aspect of an idea
conjured up as a part
of the physical realm of deception
The realm of duality
The realm of time

If the value of something exists
then the disvalue of something exists as well
Self does not have worth
Self does not have value
It already is
All That Is
beyond value and worth

There is no price tag on Eternal's worth

Switch the words
from self-worth to being worthy of Self
which you already are

Nothing to yearn or strive for
Nothing for others to recognize
Always in the Now

Know you are worthy of Self
and all the gifts of love it bestows upon you

This is your birthright

All time exists in the Now

You can focus on the past
and live the story that has always been
or
You can focus on the future
and live the story of your desire's Becoming

However
both are lived in the Now

Focus is what brings you into the moment

What brings you into the moment is directed attention
from your senses and breath
Mindfulness

Then the moment discloses:

The timeless Now
is Always

SACRED REFLECTION

Is now, all that is?

No
All That Is
is Now

Accomplishment
is not the accumulation of things or status

Things and status reside in the flux of time
Fleeting
One moment here
the next moment gone

Within the moment
lies the true meaning of success

Joy and love are the ingredients for success

True progress is measured by how much
joy and love you are experiencing

Not by how many things you accumulate
or
by the false measurement of social value

Full of success
is full of
Love and peace
Gratitude and joy
Confidence and trust

Full of Success
is full of Ultimate Purpose

Enjoy the continuous triumphs of accomplishment
of being your True Self

The cells of the body are always at attention
even when you are not
They never have moments of forgetfulness

In your moments of forgetfulness
the atoms remain constant
Receiving and preforming their job or *dharma*
On the day and night shift always

They listen to the vibration of your thoughts
and the frequencies of your feelings
And do what good cells do
Like good soldiers
They follow suit

A few main cells take the lead for others to follow
creating the body of intention
An intention that is set consciously or unconsciously
The cells do not discriminate
Like good soldiers
they obey the orders

When enough cells come together in formation
the body displays the intention in physical form

Be a good general
Be the leader
you have a whole army waiting for your command

If it is marching in a direction that is not pleasing
you have the authority to change its course

DIVINE OBSERVATION ON THE FUTURE

There was a middle-aged woman who always felt something was missing. She was always looking for something outside of herself in hopes of feeling better. Feelings of incompleteness enveloped her—always yearning to feel complete and at peace.

One night she fell asleep and had a dream. But this dream was different from any other dream she had ever experienced. It was vivid and lucid. She was awake in the dream and it seemed so real.

In the dream, she was climbing the side of a steep mountain. She started in the late afternoon and the sun was getting close to the horizon. It was a very strenuous hike. And a few times during the hike, she doubted if she would be able to make it to the top. She considered turning around. However, something was driving her and she decided to listen to the Drive.

When she got to the top, she was surprised by an older woman with a bright red shirt and a small white dog on her lap, both sitting on a boulder. The woman and dog had looks of anticipation, as though they knew she was coming. The older woman's grey hair looked beautiful against the red shirt. She looked familiar, but the middle-aged woman could not place where she knew her from and asked, "Do I know you?"

The older woman laughed and said, "Look more closely." Then she said, with a great big smile, "You did it!"

Standing on the summit, the middle-aged woman had an expansive view. She felt she was standing on top of the world: the scenery was incredible. For the first time, she felt complete and at peace. It was getting dark and she said, "I wish I had started the hike earlier."

"Be happy that you are here now," stated the older woman

with the red shirt. They looked into each other's eyes and at that moment, the dreaming woman suddenly woke up from her deep sleep and realized who the older woman was. She jumped out of bed and kissed her dog. She put on her red shirt and embraced the day with a full heart.

WISDOM SPEAKS

What we all are looking and yearning for
is right here
Right now

Once realized
The looking becomes Seeing
Seeing sees itSelf
And the past and future dissolve into the Now

⌒☙⌒

When talking to another
follow close attention to both conversations
Be mindful
Be Present
Be the speaker and the listener as well

This is good way to know what is truly being said
by you and the other

⌒⌒

Holding the future as being *in the future*
will always result in a non-reachable experience

The future exists in the desire
The desire exists in the Now
The only way it becomes reachable
and for it to manifest in the physicality
is to know
it is Here not there

When your feelings
thoughts and beliefs are living *the future*
in the Now
the matrix of its Becoming starts to form
The body needs to adjusts
from the fine vibration of energy
to the dense vibration of physicality
This adjustment is the joy of the journey

The future is not separate from you
The separateness is in believing that it is separate
This may be a hard concept to understand

The future is the expansion of the Now

It is like holding a rubber band in your hands
The expansion always exists in the rubber band

The future
like the rubber band
always exists in the Now
All you have to do is pull on it

Future and past
are different perspectives of the Now

Both in the vortex of the Present
All that exists
exists in the Present

The future and past
are different perspectives
of what already Is

⌘

A SACRED MOMENT:
THE FUTURE

We think of the future as something outside of ourselves. Something not yet reachable. Let me remind you, if you have a past memory, you are remembering it Now. If you have a dream of the future, you are imagining it Now. All there is… is Now. The future is not something to *get to*, it is something to *allow into*; allow it into your circumstance.

Most of us experience the senses of smell, taste, touch, seeing, and hearing. When we hear a bird singing, we do not go to the song, the song comes to us. If we feel the wind on our face, we do not go and seek the wind, the wind comes to us. And so on, with all that we sense.

The future and past are just different perspectives within the Now. Once you have a thought or desire of a future circumstance, it automatically starts forming vibrationally. Beliefs and feelings align and cooperate with the thoughts and actions, to open the pathways for the desired circumstance to come to you.

Think about it: when the future is experienced, it is Now. Over *there* is always *here* when experienced, for when you are there, you are here. Be the future and embrace it with all your Heart and allow the experience of the fine vibrations of thought to form into the dense vibrations of matter. The future will come to you, as the sweet sounds of the bird songs do, all within the present. By having this knowledge, the future is always present— Now is the only place to Be.

CONTEMPLATION

Close your eyes, inhale and exhale deeply for three cycles or more. When you feel settled and centered, ask yourself the question:

What does my future hold?

Will it be one of happiness, joy, accomplishment, excitement, living your passions and dreams, health, abundance, service, prosperity, peace, unity, and love?

Next, contemplate, eyes still closed, about what you would like to create in your life: health, exciting career, loving relationships, peace of mind, service, joy, and/or spiritual consciousness. For example, having a body with full energy and health, or having a career you enjoy and feel passionate about, or expressing your talents through art and music. As well as living a conscious, meaningful life.

Once you have a few thoughts and ideas, inhale and exhale deeply, then breathe normally. Focus on the inhalation and exhalation of your breath and sit in silence for a minute or two.

JOURNAL

Slowly open your eyes. Take a few minutes and jot down what you can do today that will support your desires. If you want a new career, do some research and exploration in the area. If you want health, change some eating habits and meditate. If you want peace, go into nature and be mindful. If you want to serve, donate some time or money to those in need: children, adults, animals, nature, and environment. Start with some simple steps and realize nothing is in the way of your future, but you.

You can do this practice daily or as often as your wish: clarity and direction will surface. Live your future Now. Be your future and your future will Be. Remember, *the future is Now*.

❦

6

FOLLOW HEART'S DIRECTION

In every circumstance
the Heart lovingly leads you in one direction only—Inward

The Heart is the distance to travel
It has no barriers
Especially
when there is no interference
from the personal mind

Heart is what everyone and everything
is deeply and intimately connected with
And its presence is always known

Humans and animals
plants and insects
and even inanimate objects feel the energy of Heart
All adjusting to its vibration

It speaks in the language of love
It moves from the action of inspiration
It beats to the rhythm of Consciousness

Follow Heart's Direction
It is always pointing Inward

Life's journey touches many Hearts

And to know how far you can go
is to know how near you really are

Focus on Heart and Spirit
not human frailties

Heart and Spirit
is where Self resides

To put Self first
does not mean putting you and others last
It means with each thought and action
your intention is aligned with Eternal Self

To put Self first is to put love first
compassion first
caring first
kindness and appreciation first

It is the loving relationship
with your Inner Being
A direct line with Higher Self
which some call God

When Self is first
The entirety of existence is first

Do not fear

When Self is first
the only thing left behind is ignorance

To really love
one has to be in Acceptance
Leaving no room for denial

Acceptance of Self
is the reservoir where love flows
Washing away all traces of fear

Acceptance is a state of Being
embracing your True Self

When self accepts Self
there is no distinguishing
And love flows freely
to every aspect of life

Acceptance is the door
Always open

Denial slams the door shut
with locks and chains

Infuse food with love and attention
by being mindful when eating or drinking

An Awareness will arise
and adjust to the Consciousness of what is being ingested
The ingested can then align to what is best for your body

When drinking a glass of water
and your thoughts are on the past or future
the Consciousness of water has no direction
It will not hydrate your body
It will pass through quickly
not penetrating where it is required

The water has no awareness of its function
Just like the way you drank it

When drinking a glass of water
and your thoughts are focused within the Present
the Consciousness of water has direction
Flowing where it is required
Lovingly nourishing your body

The water has awareness of its function
Just like the way you drank it

Now
the water and you
are on the same mission:

To benefit the Being with love

Overly concerned for others
is not selfless
it is feeling less of self

Too much importance and attention on others
is another way of saying you do not deserve
the importance or attention for yourself
It is also another way of avoiding

Be selfish by loving and knowing Self
through yourself
It is a priority

Heart knows this

Give yourself attention
and feel the warmth from love

For once it is known
only then can it be given

SACRED REFLECTION

What will my hands do in the world?

Hands have two sides
The palm and the back
representing the duality of the world

Hands write kind loving words or hurtful hateful words
Hands care for plants and animals or destroy them
Hands hold the light or smother the light

Hands give or take
Hands create a beautiful and caring world or
an ugly and indifferent world

Please acknowledge:

What your hands do
is solely in your hands

✧

DIVINE OBSERVATION ON LONGING

A nun in a monastery, dedicated to her religious order, had a very active mind. She was always thinking of what to do next or what she had already done. Always planning, always in mind. She felt that she had to perform certain actions to attain God's connection and approval. What she was seeking was not in the mind.

She would constantly think, "Ok, what should I do next, collect money, feed the poor, clean the monastery? I should be prepared for when God comes." The nun would repeat this statement in her mind over and over. "I should be prepared for when God comes," not knowing that a crowded mind has no space for God to enter. "I want everything to be perfect," she said to herself.

The nun waited and waited for years. Thinking about *the doing* she hoped would bring *the Being* of God. Nothing changed, other than she became more and more tired of waiting.

Every night she would look up to the heavens where she thought God resided. Every night she fell asleep with a longing in her Heart.

WISDOM SPEAKS

Thinking God is outside of you
will result in an endless search
Leaving you confused and empty

It is not in the doing
It is not in the thinking
It is not in the approving

Do you want to meet God?

Wash your dishes with all your Heart
with focused thoughts and feelings

This will put you in
direct alignment with love
Being present in Presence

Presence is
patiently waiting for you

What you are seeking
is Seeking You

To have Faith
does not mean blindly surrendering to circumstance
with the illusion
all will be fine
This gives circumstance the power

To have Faith
means surrendering to Eternal Source
with the knowledge
All is Well
This gives Eternal Source the power

A fine distinction is required
within the shift of power
Externally or Internally

Focus on the external
allows the momentum of a vibrational entity
with no direction

Focus on the Internal
allows the frequency of Heart and Soul
with love's direction

Faith is powerful
but it is important to know where the power lies

Things taken for granted
are those things
whose importance is not noticed
until they are taken away

In the moment of their absence
the true importance is realized

The simple things that support life
are often overlooked in an abusive and entitled nature

The simple acts of walking and talking
of seeing and hearing
of tasting and feeling
of breathing and smelling

The simple convenience of drinking clean water
and eating nutritious food
A warm home and a soft bed to sleep in
The joy of laughing and ones who share your love

Take one of these away
and the realization of their importance
will hit you like a ton of bricks
And on bended knee
you will be praying for their return

Appreciate your life
for when this is taken
you will not even have a knee to pray on

One must be childlike
to enter the Inner Kingdoms

As adults we have forgotten
how to laugh at the silly and play in the earth

Have fun
not abuse
Run in the wind
And allow the senses to embrace you
and the joy in your Heart to move you

Bring back the innocence of a child
Innocence is the opening to the wonder of life
and remembering how to
trust and believe again

We are mortal and immortal Beings
We sometimes do not know how to choose

We see death all around
Yet
we feel we will live forever

Both are true
The force of *I AM*
comes from the Eternal
The energy of the personal *I am*
comes from the temporary

Omnipresent mind and the infinite
are composed of Spirit and Soul
called immortality
The personal mind and the finite
are composed of the ego and body
called mortality

This is why we are so confused
Embrace them both
Eternity will present itself
if just for a moment
This allows the mortal to experience the immortal

But know
the body is needed to experience the world's mural
To experience the here and now
along with the awareness
of the before and after

When you wake up in the morning
be thankful for another day
for thousands of people did not wake up with you

Wrap your arms around the temporary
and enjoy the fleeting moments to feel
and be alive

Let go of the insanity
of misplaced thinking
The misplaced thinking of living your physical life
as though it will last forever

Appreciate the temporariness of your life
while living in the body

Be amazed
and each day will be amazing

When you are firm in your beliefs
and they are unshakable and true to you
Know
it is your truth *only*

When your realization is from your own insights
it is an expression from your Greater Perception
holding the enduring ocean of Eternal Truth

It does not make a difference what others believe
there is enough water for all
Your beliefs found the way to you
In the depths of You
Be joyous

Contrary to when you are not firm in your beliefs
because you adapted them from others
claiming their truth to be yours
These beliefs are shaky and filled with doubt
The doubt creates cracks

You attempt to glue the cracks
with religious dogma and rules
All rooted in fear and judgment
Attempting to convince others to your way

*When your beliefs are not yours
your truth is not yours*

When your realization is not from your own insights
it is a borrowed perception
and cannot even hold a drop of water

⤝⧂

Listen to the Sacred Direction

When your Heart is open
your mind is open

Open to receive the
guidance from the Higher Realms
in the language of love

Love is when you see your Self in the Other
No matter who or what is standing in front of you

Each beat of Heart is a Coded Message
for you only

Yet
the Coded Message is embedded within all of humanity

❦

A SACRED MOMENT: HEART'S DIRECTION

The heart of the physical body is in the center of the chest; it represents the center of Consciousness and the pulse of life. The Heart of Consciousness is where the human and spirit gently embrace. The mind always looks for Heart's direction, for they are intimately connected.

However, when the mind is crowded with thoughts of fear, anxiety, memories, or constant chatter, there is no space for the Heart's direction to enter. Therefore, Heart and mind coherence is interrupted and awareness is blocked. If a box is filled to its limit, nothing else can be added. If your mind is crowded with thoughts, awareness cannot enter.

I once heard an analogy of a fish tank representing a crowded mind. If you had a fish tank with a light bulb inside the tank, and you disturbed and messed up the bottom of the tank, all the debris would cloud the water. The clouded water would prevent you from seeing the light source or where it was coming from. Once the debris settled back down to the bottom, you could then see the light source clearly. When thoughts are swirling around aimlessly, the mind, like the fish tank, becomes cloudy and the Light from Heart's direction cannot be seen. Once thoughts settle, awareness fills the mind and you can now see the Light—literally.

Mind is like a lucid container: when it is not filled with undirected thoughts, the boundaries of the container melt. Your mind and Heart become one powerful unit. Heart directing mind and mind directing your thoughts—Allow Heart to wear the crown.

CONTEMPLATION

Close your eyes, inhale and exhale deeply for three cycles or more. When you feel settled and centered, ask yourself the question:

What does my Heart long for?

Listen to your Heart: does it long for love of self, love from another, peace, understanding, belonging, acceptance, purpose, joy, meaning, and connection to your Eternal Self?

Next, contemplate, with eyes still closed, what your Heart desires to experience in your life. Place one hand over the other on your heart center, in the middle of your chest. Inhale and exhale deeply from the heart center, and ask, "What does my Heart long for?" For instance, your longing may be living your life as your True Authentic Self and knowing Purpose. Maybe your Heart longs to experience a loving relationship, feeling joy, or having a peaceful mind.

Once you have a few thoughts and ideas from your contemplation, inhale and exhale deeply, then breathe normally. Focus on the inhalation and exhalation of your breath and sit in silence for a minute or two.

JOURNAL

Slowly open your eyes. Take a few minutes and jot down what your Heart truly longs for. What is it that feels incomplete and wants to feel complete and whole? This is a loaded question and may need some time to get to the core of the longings. Start simply.

You can do this practice daily or as often as you wish: clarity and direction will surface. Continue your day or evening and *follow Heart's direction*.

PART 2

EXHALE

Once awakened
you will never be able to sleep again

7

COCOON OF ILLUSION

Break through the dark cocoon
and fly

The dark cocoon
of Life's illusion

The ancients spoke about it
and labeled it
Maya

However
there is a misinterpretation

To say the experience of life is not real
is true and not true

The subtle distinguishing
lives within both

It has to do with sensations
beliefs and thoughts
All wrapped up in bundles of frequencies
of vibration and perception

All within you:
You see a tree
Hear a bird singing
Feel the breeze on your face
Taste the juice of sweet fruit
Smell the aroma of fresh baked bread
The Heart swelling from love's emotion

All these sensations are experienced
No doubt about it
Including all circumstances of your world

The questions are:
Where are they being experienced?
Who is experiencing them?

You are the Experiencer
experiencing the Experience
All within the body
All within You

However
it appears to be outside of the body
Separate from you
This is the illusion the ancient ones spoke of

Exhale and let go

The illusion is not that life is not real
the illusion is believing it is separate from you

⁘

Thoughts are snapshots
of still frames

Flickering faster than the speed of light
Connecting to other snapshots
with belief's perception
to keep them in motion

Therefore
creating Life's moving picture
of circumstance

Similar to the mechanics of movie making

The concept of a motionless movement
of the still frames of thought
is difficult to comprehend
It is beyond the mind

Allow the insight of its functioning
from the Sight of higher realms

And know
for change in circumstance to occur
the whole stream of snapshots in your life's movie
does not have to change

All that has to change is
one snapshot at a time

⸙

To feel the essence of Life
appreciate those little
seemingly unimportant things

Those circumstances and situations
that are often overlooked
What you are seeking
is seeking you
Calling for your attention
moment by moment

Whether you are washing the dishes
or tending to the garden

Whether you are eating dinner
or spending time with loved ones

Whether you are meditating
or bathing your child

Appreciate
those little
seemingly unimportant things
encompassing your life

They will expose the Secret

You see
within those little
seemingly unimportant things
are those big
genuinely important things

Sitting by the ocean

Seeing the water
Hearing the seagulls
Tasting the salt
Smelling the beach
Feeling the breeze

A Shift Occurs
Mindfulness within Mindlessness

Seeing through sight
Hearing through sound
Tasting through saltiness
Smelling through scent
Feeling through touch

All the senses merge into One Feeling
One Feeling merges into
One Experience

The Experience of what is truly being Experienced
Self encountering Self

As the Universe is limitless
so are you

To believe in limitation is limitation

Your limitlessness is only limited
by allowing limitation to exist

For within our limitlessness
All is allowed
even limitation

Know:
Your vastness
is as far and deep
as you possibly can imagine
Plus
so much more

We all have learned
the physical world is made-up of atoms

And atoms are mostly space
dancing to the music of vibration
and the pull of frequency

Thought is vibration's point of origin
and it strengthens with the frequency of *belief-feelings*
Directed by desires and focus

Every aspect of existence:
from the atom to the universe
from the rock to the mountain
from the ant to the elephant
from the weed to the tree
from a speck of dust to the human
is fueled by Source's Light
Projecting the Whole Image of itSelf onto the World's Screen

No matter how many fragments and segments
that seem to exist in the world
each one contains the Whole Image

And with keen Sight
the experience of the True Essence of existence is known

Be mindful

The *Whole* is in every *part* of life
The part could not exist
without the Whole

Within every encounter and circumstance
Within every object and being
lives the Whole

The apple
a part
could not exist without the tree
the whole

And the tree
the whole
could not exist without the apple seed
the part

The part and whole are
the Whole Part

Supreme purpose is revealed in
every feature of life
Always exposing its entirety

Even when the part appears to be defective
the Whole will expose the perfection

This is the knowledge the wise live by

Break out of the dark panic
and direct your thoughts
You are the master
not the servant

Breaking the cycle of *thought-energy*
may be difficult at first

Embrace your human-self
It is the vehicle for Eternal Self to be known
Acknowledge both
but know who is in charge

You cannot see the light
until you acknowledge the dark

One's own thoughts
are one's own world

When the body perishes
self merges with Self in Total Awareness
Finite melts into Infinite

Make your world a good one

You only reign over your kingdom
as long as your body lasts

Time
is a tricky concept

It rules our lives
Tick tock
Running and trying to beat the clock
But
what is it?
Time is not something to hold on to
Impossible to do
The past is a memory
The future is imagination
All within the timeless Now

Thinking is always thinking about the past or future
This is why you cannot figure things out by thinking
Thinking crowds the mind's space
Leaving no room to Receive

When thinking ceases for a few moments
things will be figured out
Have you ever noticed that?

We have to use the whole Mind
Personal and Higher
to be a whole Being

The personal mind abides by time
An aspect of the illusion

The Higher Mind is timeless and eternal
and knows only Now
An aspect of Ultimate Reality

⌒⌒

The mirage in the desert of Life's illusion
Thirsting for the quench of the Eternal
Seeking the safety from the Eternal
Desiring love from the Eternal
Embracing joy with the Eternal
Knowing Purpose
Seeing the Beauty

This is what we are all seeking

The oasis can never be reached
within the illusion the desert presents
The body will always be crying out
to quench its thirst

Similarly
The outside world can never be reached
within the illusion the physical world presents
The Being will always be crying out
to quench its thirst

How do you quench the thirst for the Eternal?

Always drink from the fountain Within
The Eternal Oasis
The never-ending flow of your True Essence

SACRED REFLECTION

How can I touch the world?

You cannot touch the midst of the outside world
It is translucent and holds no substance

The nature of the world appears to consist
of matter
Independent from you

Through investigation
matter cannot be found
It is 99.9% space

Where is the world we share reside?
Certainly
not outside of ourselves

You have tried so many times
You are looking in the wrong direction

The real in reality resides in your Inner Experience
And the only way to touch the outside world
is from the inside

Once the trance of the real in reality
loosens

Once the misconception
of the permanent in the temporary
fades

And

Once the blurry vision
of the separateness in Oneness
sharpens

Total responsibility for your life and the world
comes into focus
Along with empowerment
insight and joy

Appreciation and gratitude become your true partners
revealing the transient nature of life

Your thinking wraps you in the cocoon of darkness
or breaks you free with wings of flight

Thoughts work for you or against you

You are the Director

When you are not directing with focus
thoughts will take direction
from someone or something else

And pull from the surrounding environment
whatever is in the Mass Mind
sticking to you like fly paper
Being at the mercy of whatever is attracted

Be the Master of your own Mind
Take flight and see the world from the Heights
and all will make sense

⌒⌒⌒

SACRED OBSERVATION ON THE ILLUSION OF LIFE

A man lay on his death bed, staring at the fluorescent lights flickering on and off, on and off. "Similar to my life," he thought. He started reflecting on his family, work, and life in general. "What does this all mean?" he said to himself with limited breath, and started coughing until his lungs hurt.

He was an angry man and felt the world was against him. He had to work hard for every penny he made and never wanted to let any of it go. He did not talk to his family for years; he felt disrespected and trusted no one. The only thing he trusted was his made-up story of his life. He lived every day as though life was a battlefield: permanent and real.

The nurse came in the room, smiled and asked if he needed anything. He barked back and said, "What do you think I need? I'm dying. What can I possibly want at this stage of my life?"

The nurse gazed back with compassionate eyes and fixed his bed. Her caring and love was felt deep within him. Suddenly, a light flashed from within the man, the realization that his existence will be no more. He felt at peace and filled with gratitude for the last moments of his life. He smiled for the first time in years.

He reached for the nurse's hand and said, "Thank you."

WISDOM SPEAKS

Appreciate every moment of your life
This is where the Light is seen
The Sacred Knowledge

Staying in the dark of ignorance is faulty living
Never seeing the True Beauty of Life

Eventually
the True Beauty will be realized

And you may smile in recognition
of the wonderful illusion
called life

Searching
Always searching

Not feeling at Home

There is always an uncomfortable feeling
lurking by your side
as if forgetting some important
unanswered questions

Always looking for Home
The feelings of completeness
love and belonging

All the money
All the relationships
All the creations
All the success
will not open the door

Knocking from the outside
Always knocking

Step over the Threshold

Awake
You are not of this world

It is just a visit

A SACRED MOMENT:
LIFE'S ILLUSION

You may have heard that life is an illusion, which yogis call Maya. What does illusion really mean? If you get burned, the pain certainly does not feel like an illusion: it hurts! Your family, friends, animals, and circumstances certainly do not feel like an illusion. You touch, see, hear, taste, smell, and experience the sensations from your senses. So where is the illusion? The illusion comes from the premise that your life's experiences are separate from you and outside of yourself.

If you see a tree, where are you seeing it? If you hear a bird sing, where are you hearing it? If you feel the caress of the wind on your face, where are you feeling it? All sensations and experiences occur within you. And most importantly, they are interpreted by you. The illusion the ancient ones speak of is thinking the experiences and sensations are outside and separate from you—believing the world you consider reality is permanent and real. What we are really seeing is our construct of perception: *The Seen is for the benefit of the Seer.*

The good news is that with a shift of perception and interpretation, you can change unwanted circumstances— all within your focus. One way to have a shift of perception is through appreciation and gratitude. Appreciation and gratitude will shed Light on circumstances: they both are experienced within the present moment only. In the present moment, love is felt and brings a direct connection to your Eternal Self, lasering through the veil of Maya—Seeing Self in the other, whether it be a person, animal, plant, thing, landscape, or circumstance. Seeing Self in the other, one falls in love with all of existence.

Come out of the cocoon and fly with this Secret close to your Heart.

CONTEMPLATION

Close your eyes, inhale and exhale deeply for three cycles or more. When you feel settled and centered, ask yourself the question:

Am I appreciating my life?

Are you appreciating the air you breathe, your home, senses, family, friends, animal partners, a warm bed, food to eat, and the blue sky? Do you live with the realization that life is temporary and not meant to be taken for granted? The list to cultivate appreciation and gratitude in your life is endless.

Next, contemplate, eyes still closed, the aspects of your life you can appreciate, recognizing the full worth of your life. There is always something you can appreciate: the breath that gives your body life or sleeping on a soft bed, the love of friends and family, a sunny day, good food and the beauty of a flower.

For example, eating a meal with full mindfulness and tasting every morsel, or seeing the light in a child's eyes, or walking on the street enjoying the breeze and the sweet smell of flowers in the air— all exist within the state of appreciation and gratitude.

Once you have a few ideas and thoughts, inhale and exhale deeply, then breathe normally. Focus on the inhalation and exhalation of your breath and sit in silence for a minute or two.

JOURNAL

Slowly open your eyes. Take a few minutes and jot down some things you feel grateful for and appreciate in your life. Be mindful during the day of what you wrote in your journal and cultivate the state of appreciation in your everyday activities.

You can do this practice on a daily basis or as often as you wish: clarity and direction will surface. Go out into the world and live your life with full appreciation and awareness: break out of the *cocoon of illusion*.

8

THE SHADOW IS THAT WHICH BLOCKS THE LIGHT

The Light shows who you are
The Dark speaks of what you can Become

When fear surfaces and the Dark Shadow
grabs your throat and stomach
it reminds you about the *you*
you do not want to see

The Dark Shadow hovers

You hide your face and ignore its presence
hoping no one can see it
But everyone does

The Dark Shadow follows
walking slightly behind you
Hearing its footsteps closing in
The fear is monstrous

The dark side seems to remind you of the *lesser than*
Beliefs of unworthiness and defectiveness
weakness and shame
Beliefs created during childhood interpretations
of neglect and betrayal
abandonment and abuse
Disguised as truth

Why does it come up now?
Because you are now ready to face it

When you were younger
the dark side took your pain
You were too young to handle the intensity

The Dark Shadow was your friend and protected you

Now
as an adult
the dark shows the light

It is time to face your Dark Shadow
It is here not to remind you of your *lesser than*
It is here to show you the way to your *more than*

The light shows who you are
The dark shows who you can become

The Dark Shadow whispers first
then speaks

If not heard
it yells
If still not heard
it will act out
Wanting to be set free

It has done its job
now do yours

Looking
into the eyes of another
can be difficult indeed
Whether you like them or not

Once the eyes lock
the awareness surfaces

Through the eyes of the other
You are looking back at you

Feeling exposed

Now
you are face-to-face with yourself
no matter who or what is in front of you

The question arises:
Are you ready to take on this responsibility?

As the night covers all
the stars peek through

The darker it becomes
the more stars are revealed

If it was not for the dark
the suns of the universe would remain hidden

Nature is beautiful
To see the true beauty of nature is to embrace it all

The flowers swaying in the wind
The leaves glowing from the sun's light
The waves of the ocean
The snow-capped mountains
As well as
a shark coming up from under the surface of the water
to feast on a young seal

The knowledge of nature's precise balance
is beyond the mind's understanding

You are beautiful

To see your true beauty is to embrace it all
The dark as well as the light
The strengths and weaknesses

The knowledge of your precise balance
is also beyond your mind's understanding

❧

Relax for a moment
Reconnect to feelings
Relief is on the way

The lighted path is just under your feet

Walk it
Move forward
Do not turn around

There is nothing
that can fill your plate from the past
It is gone

No more searching for something that is not there anymore

Walk on the forward path
holding an empty plate in hand
with excited anticipation

The excitement of the plate
being filled and emptied
over and over again

Birds singing their morning songs
Appearing to be outside
The beautiful flowers blooming in the garden
Appearing to be outside

Separate from you

The songs are heard where the flowers are seen
Find this Place

The journey within
requires silence and gratitude
awareness and allowing
Then the insight of your Magnificence
will be brought forward

This is where beauty originates
and meshes with Sacred Knowledge

Just observe
Just Be

And fall into *That*
where All gathers

Answering all your questions

⁓

The Dark Shadow speaks a familiar language

It is the language of your fears and pain
Do not turn away
Listen

Shadows tell you where and how
the Light Source is blocked

Without light
shadows would not exist
Without you
shadows would have no home

Walk on the beach
with the sun's rays on your back
and your shadow in front of you
Your shadow is always in step with you
It follows your command
Move to the right
It moves
Move to the left
It moves
You are the shadow's master
It does not have purpose of its own

The Shadow defines the light by displaying the outline
of what is blocking the rays

If the shadow is in front of you
the light is behind you

Turn around

The shadows in the physical world
and the Shadow of the spiritual world
follow similar principles

Dark Shadow speaks and projects the catalyst
to grow and expand
Light Shadow speaks of divinity and love

You are the projector and filmmaker
The film is made from your
beliefs and thoughts
feelings and choices

The Light source is the Eternal Source
Out of love
it gives you what you project

Dark Shadow gives depth of Being

Turn around and face your Dark Shadow
and let it speak of the Light

The pain of growing

The discomfort of the dark
pushing me to move

Not listening to the Invocation

Why the resistance?

Is it that I am not accepting my place?
or
Is my Place not accepting my absence?

Choose your choice

Your feelings are a clue
Choice is conscious

Choose to listen

Within the choosing
lies the creation of a new world

The train roars
A sparrow sings softly
Choose to listen to the sparrow's song

Empty beer cans cover the ground
A small daisy springs up between the cracks in the cement
Choose to talk to the daisy

The odor of car fumes
A faint fragrance of pine trees
Choose to breathe in the pine scent

A flash of the obvious

The choosing of choice
is the only choice to choose

⁓

SACRED OBSERVATION ON LIFE'S PURPOSE

A teenage boy was walking on the sidewalk. Like all teenagers, he was upset and angry about something or other. He decided to take out his frustration on the ants. He stepped and twisted his foot on every ant that crawled across the cement, making sure he smashed as many as he could.

He mumbled, "I am different and nobody likes me." He was always concerned about not having the right clothes or saying the right thing or having the right haircut. He took a moment and watched the ants. They all seemed so busy with purpose and direction: this made him even angrier.

The teenager felt power over the ants. He was just about to step on a few more ants but decided to take a closer look. He bent down onto the sidewalk and grabbed one ant with the intention of crushing it between his fingers. The ant looked right into his eyes, antennae twitching. And it seemed to be talking to him. "Shit, I must be going crazy," the teenager said to himself.

The ant spoke:

To know life's Purpose is to know your purpose
for they are one and the same
The world is supported by diversity
not by sameness
Knowing the individual is to know the collective
for they are one and the same
The world cannot give you what you do not already have
To know the world
know you
for they are one and the same

Knower
knowing and known
Seer
seeing and seen
Doer
doing and done
have no distinction
To look at another and want to be like them
negates your whole existence
To look at another to inspire what will come from you
celebrates your whole existence
The oak tree does not try to be a blade of grass
A robin does not try to be a dragonfly
If the tree didn't know and if the bird didn't know
who they are
the world would collapse
What is the world?
It is what it is by you being you

The teenager was taken aback by this experience and became totally lost in the moment; he did not even notice the people stepping over him while he was bent down on the sidewalk listening to the ant.

He loosened his grip on the ant and gently placed it back on the sidewalk. He stood up, brushed his clothes off, raised his head very high, and walked down the street with a smile.

WISDOM SPEAKS

You never know what form your teacher will come in

A shield protects from danger
Keeping one safe
Shields intercept attacks

Many religions and spiritual practices
encourage spiritual shields to fend against attacks
of negative and evil energies
Some use visualization
jewelry or even garlic to push away the vampires
Always on guard against attacks

A shield to keep out the enemy
is actually a shield that protects and holds in
anger and fear
ignorance and resistance
You are stuck in the limited space
of what the shield offers
Not a warrior
A prisoner

If you like the concept of shields
there is a shield for you

The Shield of Eternal Source

A warrior with the sword of awareness and direction from Heart
Slicing the dark and Lighting the Way
Always on the path of peace and love
A path the enemies cannot walk

It is a Shield that does not protect
yet nothing can touch you

SACRED REFLECTION

How do we handle all the negative and mean people of the world?

Wisdom sees the other as a projection of one's Self:

Embrace both the sage and the criminal
the positive-minded and negative-minded person
the kind and cruel being
Polarities must exist for life to move and grow

However
the contrast of polarities is only possible
due to the underlying Sameness of Awareness

Be the observer
in the state of Awareness always
where polarities melt
And the Direct Perception of what truly is surfaces
And what truly is
is Oneness and beauty of Self

In nature
The beauty of Self is in plain sight
Even when a mountain lion has a deer by its throat

THE DEPTHS OF HEIGHT

To reach for the heights
depth must come first
This is the dichotomy of life
The height is not known until the depth is experienced
Where neither exist
This is the paradox of life

This is a story of the paradoxical dichotomy of life:

A woman was hiking alone on a mountainous trail. She slipped off the edge of the trail and grabbed hold of a branch growing out from the side of the mountain. She was dangling between life and death. The drop was deep, and if she let go, death was inevitable. She yelled for help, but no one came. She was alone. Her thoughts raced, and she did not feel strong enough to pull herself up over the ledge— death was near. A small Voice whispered:

Dig deeply within
The strength is present

She tried and tried again and could not pull herself up. She started crying. A flower growing from a crack within the rock caught her attention. "The delicate flower found a way to push through a hard place. If the flower could do it, I can do it," she said to herself.

She used every ounce of her physical strength and more of her spiritual strength. Finally, she reached for a small extension of a rock beneath the ledge and pulled herself up. She lay on the flat surface of the mountain ledge and cried for hours.

She stood up and realized she would never have known her strength if she had not gone deeply within. She briskly walked on her way, feeling confident she could now face and handle anything. The insight surfaced:

To rise above anything
you must dig deeply
And know
the Heavens are waiting within the depths of you always

Pain and suffering
Know the distinction

Pain
alerts the human body
using physical sensations and signals
A warning through the discomfort
of the body
emotions or mind
Something has to change for relief

Pain offers the opportunity to adjust

Suffering
is the interpretation or story
you tell yourself about the pain
through thoughts and judgements
beliefs and perceptions
Something carrying heavily on your back

Suffering is a choice

Human pain will always be
Suffering is optional

Your so-called problems
are extensions of you
They are not coming *at* you
they are coming *from* you

The outer world cannot be blamed for your inner problems
Be accountable

The outer is the inner
To focus on the outer is avoiding the remedy
To focus on the inner is the remedy

Don't fear
fear
It is the messenger
It shows you what you are not

It continues to come up to remind you
what you have forgotten

Fear wants to be released
and return to love

A SACRED MOMENT:
YOUR SHADOWS

Your Dark Shadow is the compilation of all that you do not want to face—fear, hurt, pain, guilt, self-doubt, and shame. The Shadow holds all the fears from your childhood and releases it when you are ready to face them. As scary as it may seem, it did protect you when you were young by holding the intensity of the pain; it was standing by and waiting for when you are ready and prepared to face and release it.

The Light Shadow holds all your greatness, uniqueness, magnificence, and love— which you are also afraid to face. For some, the Light Shadow is more difficult to embrace than the Dark Shadow. However, both lead us to our true essence of Eternal Source, our GodSelf.

Imagine standing on the beach with the sun's rays on your back and your body's shadow in front of you, projected onto the sand. The sun is very bright and is creating a precise outline of your body on the sand. You pick up your right arm; the shadow picks up its arm. You take a step to the left; the shadow moves to the left. Play with your shadow by jumping, twirling your arms, or any other antics you desire. Witness how the shadow obeys. Then turn around and face the light of the sun, knowing the shadow cannot do anything without you— feel your mastery.

Shadows prove the light. If all of creation was light, nothing could be seen. Nothing could be felt. The Shadows offers contrast and the opportunity to thrive through experiencing the polarities of life.

CONTEMPLATION

Close your eyes, inhale and exhale deeply for three cycles or more. When you feel settled and centered, ask yourself the question:
What Dark Shadows am I running away from?

What fear, shame, guilt, pain, and beliefs are you telling yourself that are standing in the way of your full potential and not allowing your Authentic Self to come to Light?

Next, contemplate, eyes still closed, what fears, pains, shames, or hurts are lurking in the Shadow of your Soul and Being, preventing your Authentic Self to surface. Bring it to the Light Shadow by acknowledging it. For instance, if you have a fear of rejection or feelings of being unworthy of love, just acknowledge them. Acknowledgement is the beginning stage of facing your fears and beginning the journey of liberation.

Once you have a few ideas and thoughts from your contemplation, inhale and exhale deeply, then breathe normally. Focus on the inhalation and exhalation of your breath and sit in silence for a minute or two.

JOURNAL

Slowly open your eyes. Take a few minutes to recognize your Dark Shadow and jot down what fears, shames, doubts, guilts, and beliefs are casting the Shadows in your world. Next, jot down how you can become the master of your Shadow by being the master of your feelings and not feeding into your fears. Then turn to your Light and allow love of Self to surface. Just acknowledging your Dark Shadow sheds Light on it. Also, make a list of your Light Shadows including your talents, uniqueness, compassion, kindness, caring, or creative expressions.

You can do this practice daily or as often as you wish: clarity and direction will surface. And continue the day with this knowledge: *The Dark Shadow is That which blocks the Light from your Greater Self; a Shadow outlining what must be faced. Face your Shadow fearlessly and become the master you were meant to be.*

9

LIFE'S DREAM

Life is an experience
of sleeping or being awake in the Dream

We are all dreaming
the Dream of our Becoming

We can sleep in the Dream
or
be awake in the Dream

Sleeping is a hypnotic trance
of misleading impressions of the world
Not knowing the real in reality
Creating the appearance of you
being separate from the world

Awake is total awareness
of the fleeting essence of the world
Knowing the unreal in reality
With the insight of you
being One with the world

Be a lucid dreamer of life
Remaining awake while in the Dream

Once awakened
the Dream is evident
And no longer can it be hidden

Now
The Dreamer
walks into the Dream
with eyes wide open

Where does the world exist?
If the ground is wet
it is not dry
If it is day
it is not night
If it is up
it is not down

Wet is not dry
and dry is not wet
So
What is wet without the other?
What is day without the other?
What is up without the other?

What are you without the other?

The *ifs and nots* rely on each other
If it was not for the *nots*
would the world be known?

Would you be known?

The other confirms the existence of the other
Sparking the Dream
And the smoke from the spark rises and twirls
together in the dance of life

Revealing that you are not you
without the Other

We are living in the Dream
Dreams are the stuff the world is made of

How silly of us thinking the world is permanent

It all starts with a dream

And if dreamed often enough
and if believed strong enough
It spreads and infiltrates the mass consciousness
and becomes Life's Dream itself
The Dream we all share

Humanity is approaching a major shift in consciousness
knowing the real in reality
is not real at all

Collectively
we dream the real in the
Dream of Life

We are the Sacred Chalice
holding the sweet wine of all possibilities

Drink
And create a dynamic Dream

We are all in it together
Like it or not

Perfection and non-perfection
are in it together
Like it or not

Accept your human flaws
The flaws are juxtaposed to your perfection
enabling the Light to peek through

Life is a translation of vibration
from the two points of attraction
which makes it known

Up makes down known
Day makes night known
Dark makes light known
Human makes Spirit known

The flaws of a human
are not flaws at all

It is the beautiful design of the world of duality
to reveal *who you are not*
to know *who you are*

The Divine Identity of I AM
Like it or not

The false identification of the breath
is what needs to be loosened and eventually let go

This identification feels that the breath
depends on you
An unconscious perspective

Be mindful
the Force that grows your hair or takes it away
is the same Force
that moves the Earth around the sun
and *That* which moves your breath

One must develop a deep trust of this Force
Know that the movement of the breath is
independent of you
A Conscious perspective

Ultimate letting go is required
Death must occur
which brings up the fear of fears
Desperately holding on with white knuckles

But this is a death of another kind
A death of a disordered state of mind
A death of deceptive appearance
which falsely perceives and interprets

A death bringing a birth
The birth of the blessed event
Total Absorption with this Force

That which moves your breath
is That which moves all of existence

Come up from the ashes of illusion
in the Light of your True Self

Be daring
Let go of the mirage of who you think you are

Allow death
to truly live

⌒⌒

Keep up with your personal dream
It will expand into the Eternal Dream

Attempting to control and manipulate
will keep you in a limited dream of narrow sight

All you have to do is focus on your dream
Your dream only
Release and let go

And allow the Eternal Dream of its Becoming
An unlimited Dream of expansive Sight

Your dream is a projection of the Eternal Dream
An intimate affair

All individual dreams
make up the Eternal Dream
From all the kingdoms
mineral to human
From all the universes
atom to galaxy

Your Authentic Self holds your personal dream
Eternal Self holds the Eternal Dream

Listen to your Authentic Self
it is the vechicle to transport the voice of Eternal Self
Always whispering the Sacred Equation:

Dreams are not separate
Selves are not separate

The Ultimate Experience
is *That* which the flowers reach for
it is *That* which the universe revolves around
and it is *That* when our eyes meet

Swimming in an endless ocean
but not alone

To love and be loved
is the Cycle desired by all of creation

Everything stems from the Cycle
It makes the Dream
The Dream called Life

If you are abundant and happy
and feel loved
the Dream expands

If you are struggling and frustrated
and feel unloved
the Dream contracts

Look in your Dream
for the expansion of love
or
the contraction of fear

And you will know where the dream
is dreaming from

Being loved or unloved

Growth needs space

The farmer carefully spaces the plant seeds
for them to have room to grow and take form
Setting the conditions for optimum growth

The farmer does not hover over the plants
blocking the sun's light
awaiting fruition

The fruit
the plant will unveil
will only be known at the stage of fruit set
The growth is not known until it grows

The farmer holds the expectation
by witnessing only
Not interfering with the process

Plant your seeds of intention
and carefully space them
to have room to grow and take form
Setting the conditions for optimum growth

Do not hover over your desires
blocking the Light
awaiting manifestation

Expect them to grow
by witnessing only
Not interfering with the Process

Set the intention
let go and stand back

When you stand too close
you are blocking the Light
Nothing can grow
Nothing can manifest

Move out of the way
and allow the Process to do its process

Hold the expectation
intermingled with the Mystery
of not knowing what magnificent form
your intention will unveil

༚

There is a misinterpretation
of the personal mind's capabilities

When a problem arises
know it can never be figured out by thinking
The personal mind is a container
Too much thinking crowds and fills the container
Leaving no space for the infusion
for a new idea or resolution

When trying to figure things out by thinking
the same thoughts are circulating
over and over
The same thoughts that have been
blocking your way out

The personal mind is not capable of new ideas
It only perceives the idea once infused
Infused or downloaded from a Higher perspective

When mind is filled with thinking
there is no room for new ideas

Clear your mind
Empty the container

Once you let go
the mind allows the letting In
Thus
it can now
focus on a new idea of direction

CG

SACRED REFLECTION

If life is a Dream, does anything really matter?

The point of creation
produces the interpretive-energy of the Dream state
which extends into other generations and lifetimes

A motion that appears to be moving forward
bringing a thriving and prosperous world to enjoy
or a depraved and impoverished world to suffer

The vibration of the Dream remains constant
through the interpretation of strong belief
and actions backing it up
The interpretation of history continues
The interpretation of god through religion continues
The Dream that life is real continues

However
the Dream's focal point springs from the Stream of Well-Being
Therefore
it is always attempting to return to that Stream
Burst the Dream to reveal its True Essence
of its returning motion with no judgment
Life becomes transparent
Does anything really matter? Yes and No
Yes...because Life's Dream continues to be experienced as being
real
bringing joy or pain to the world we share
No...because the only real in Life is
it's a Dream

Life is but a wisp of a Dream

Your temporary home

The Light from one's flame of existence
leaves an imprint on the
world's Living Picture
As well as
within the Hearts of all those
who touched the Light

Death is the awakening from the Dream
The Great Transition
of one's flame merging
with the radiant Light of the Divine

Your Everlasting Home

Make a Commitment to your Authentic Self
The Self that is an expression of Eternal Self
The word
commitment
appears to be binding
But in the mystic's world
it is allegiance to Supreme Consciousness

When you are committed to being uncommitted
You are committed to the very place you thought
commitment would lead to
Imprisonment

In a prison cell with a neon sign directing to the exit
However
choosing to stay in the whirlwind of searching

Running away from Commitment is running away from love
Running away from love is running away from freedom

Commitment to Authentic Self will guide you through your
commitment to the world
Placing focus on your dedication
to following your passions and true feelings
Unveiling who you are
within every circumstance and experience

Complete devotion and conviction to Eternal Self
is a priority

The road to freedom is through Commitment

SACRED OBSERVATION ON BEING AWAKE

One day a woman was sitting in her kitchen, realizing she needed to play more. She was much too serious about her life, very involved in the drama of her family and workplace. Her thoughts repeated the same scenario of the drama— with no way out.

"When was the last time I had fun?" she whispered to herself. "I am not sure if I even know how to have fun anymore." Her eyes closed and she fell into a deep sleep.

When she woke from her sleep, she looked out the window and to her surprise the ground was covered in deep snow. It was beautiful. The snow-covered ground glistened as if diamonds covered the landscape. The steady downward spiral of snowflakes put her in a hypnotic state for a moment. She was very excited and quickly got dressed, put on her snow boots, and went outside. She felt like a child again.

She had an impulse to make a snowwoman. She meticulously started making the body, rolling a big ball of snow for the base and carefully placing a smaller ball on top for the torso, and another smaller ball for the head—the snow was perfect for packing. She picked a place where she could see it from all angles of her yard and most importantly, from her kitchen window. She completed the body and she stood back to assess the snowwoman. "Yes, buttons for the eyes, carrot for the nose (hoping the horses would not eat it) and M&M candies for a smiling mouth." She was having so much fun, her seriousness melted away and time was nonexistent. She felt awake.

She decided to put a scarf around the neck of the snowwoman and a cowgirl hat on its head. "I will give her a name." Suddenly she looked at her watch. "Oh! I need to go—I'll finish when I come back," she joyfully said to herself.

She left for a little while and could not wait to return and continue making the snowwoman. While she was away the sun came out, the sun's rays beat on the snow figure. When she came back, there was a pile of half melted snow with the scarf and hat laying on top. She felt sad for moment. "I should have finished it first before leaving," she said solemnly. She picked up the hat and scarf and even threw a few M&M's in her mouth to remember the sweetness of the moment and slowly walked away.

WISDOM SPEAKS

Nothing lasts too long
it is the design of the physical life
Not knowing this
is when one is asleep
and takes life for granted

Life is for a moment only

Appreciate the moment
Be mindful of the moment
Be joyful in the moment

It is the only way to live

Dreams cannot hold anything
They are the translucent haze of the story
we tell ourselves

Yet

Dreams hold everything
They are the Spark
for the main Essence of creation

⌒⊙⌒

A SACRED MOMENT:
SLEEPING IN THE DREAM

Life is a Dream in a constant state of Becoming. When we are not aware or conscious of the impermanence of life, we do not acknowledge the True Essence of existence. We are in a dream state living our physical existence as though it is real. How can life be real when it is temporary, transient, and fleeting? Life is a short visit: enjoy every moment.

When you fall asleep and you experience a vivid or lucid dream, it seems so real. However, when you awake, you realize it was just a dream. But the magical essence lingers. Life, too, is a wisp of a dream. The Awakened State is living in the Present, not engaging in the sorrow of the past or the anxiety of the future. And once awakened, you will never take your life for granted — for the real in existence is exposed. And the real you thought was real— is no longer. Awake! Bathe in the wonder of it all.

CONTEMPLATION

Close your eyes, inhale and exhale deeply for three cycles or more. When you feel settled and centered, ask yourself the question:

If life is a fleeting essence, what am I holding on to so tightly?

Are you holding on to material things, people, ideas, fear, time, or yearnings? Are you holding on to beliefs about yourself: beliefs of being unworthy, shame, fear, or guilt? What are you holding on to, not enabling you to be in the Present and not being able to enjoy and love your life? Are you allowing addictive thinking to be more important than being in the Present Moment?

Next, contemplate, eyes still closed, what you are holding on to that is blocking your Authentic Self to come forth. What is truly important to you? What is everlasting? Being Present will expose what is truly important to you and keep you from falling prey to old belief patterns blocking your joy.

Be present with your loved ones, truly listen to what is being said and look into their eyes. And most importantly, love yourself, forgive yourself, and embrace yourself. Also, be present with all the activities required of you, such as cooking, cleaning, working, and talking. Feel the Life Force instead of the scattering energy of your thoughts getting in the way of a fulfilling life. By being in the Present Moment, the clarity of your priorities will sharpen.

Once you have a few thoughts and ideas on what beliefs you feel are blocking your joy, inhale and exhale deeply, then breathe normally. Focus on the inhalation and exhalation of your breath and sit in silence for a minute or two.

JOURNAL

Slowly open your eyes. Take a few moments and jot down what you are holding on to so tightly that interferes with your joy and appreciation of life. Where are your thoughts most of the time? Past or future? Worry or fear? By being aware of your thoughts you can bypass the conditioning and habits of addictive thinking and replace them with positive and new belief patterns—opening to new pathways of perception. Make two lists: on one side write down what interferes with your joy; next to it, write down how you can replace it with something that can bring you joy. For example, if you worry, replace it with ways of expressing gratitude. If you have guilt, replace it with ways of expressing self-compassion and forgiveness. Of course, this is just a start to uncovering what blocks your true joy, but it is a good start.

You can do this practice daily or as often as you wish: clarity and direction will surface. Go out into the world with full appreciation of the transitory essence of life to be awake in *Life's Dream*.

10

The Eyes Do Not See

You see through the lenses of belief

The aspect of Seeing has nothing to do with
the physical eyes

The eyes are vessels sending images to the brain
The images are actually upside down

Maybe that is why we are all so confused

The images are turned right-side up
by *tightly-knitted interpretations*

Interpretations derived from beliefs and thoughts
the lenses which the images filter through

Deeply grooved from the beginning of time
passed down from generation to generation

We may all agree it is a mountain
But we may not all agree
on how we *see* the mountain

The multitude of aspects and circumstances
existing in the physical world
are perceived and experienced by
the multitude of interpretations

Seeing
is from your Inner Vision
and determines the meaning of your reality

Perception and interpretation are intimately linked

Once your interpretation
changes
your perception changes

Once your perception
changes
your world changes

There is no *real* in reality
other than what you project onto the World's Screen
and believe it to be real

The eyes are windows
allowing you to See
the perception of the world
you are projecting

⌒⌒

Pity not
the sad
poor or dying

Pity sets you far apart
as though these circumstances
cannot touch you

Pity views from the outside
standing on a pedestal

Look upon the sufferer as yourself
Do not to take the suffering as yours
just embrace and feel for the other

Pity will transform into compassion
Compassion moves into action

Compassion views from the inside
standing on equal ground

Compassion shares the experience
as a support for the other

Pity looks from a judgmental eye
Compassion feels from Heart

Judging sees the many
A feeling Heart knows only One

Awareness
is beyond looking

Looking implies
there is *a you*
looking at the *other*

Whereas
Awareness witnesses *You*
in the *Other*

Awareness is the Eye of the Seer
The Seer is not a thing or person
It is the perspective from the power of Seeing

It appears to see through the mind
The mind is where separation exists
However
Seeing is seeing itself in all Experiences

The Seen is for the benefit of the Seer

Therefore
no separation
All is just witnessed
Embrace this insight

There is nothing to see
other than
the Seer
Seeing and Seen are One
with no distinction

DIVINE OBSERVATION ON INTERPRETATION

"Rain, I hate the rain. It's ruining my day," stated a man running frantically to his job holding a newspaper over his head, attempting to dodge the raindrops. As he ran, he stepped into a puddle and mud splashed onto his new pants. "Damn!" he yelled, with a frown wrinkling his forehead.

An older woman sitting on a bench said, "Are you all right?"

"Yes, yes, I just hate the rain, it ruins everything... look at me! I am a mess, I have an important meeting at work, what will they think?"

She smiled and said, "Sit with me."

"What? In the rain?" he said with a confused look on his face.

"Yes, in the rain," she said with a smile.

He felt defeated and sat by her side.

"You see the drops of water on the leaves and how the flower petals all seem to soak it up? All seem a bit brighter and fuller, wouldn't you agree?" She smiled as she spoke.

At that moment, a bird sipped from a small puddle and lifted its head for the drops of water to trickle down its throat and enter its tiny body. It tweeted with delight and flew off.

"Take a moment, my son, look at the light and music the rain brings."

At first, he thought she was crazy. He looked around and to his surprise, all did seem to glitter and the sound of the raindrops became sweet music to his ears. He lifted his face to the sky and felt the drops on his face.

He felt something had changed. He looked at his pants and said, "They don't seem so bad. I am sure everyone will understand it is raining outside."

The older woman looked into his eyes and said, "What changed? The rain? Or how you *see* the rain?"

He looked at her and smiled in acknowledgment, thanked her, and walked to work with a great big smile on his face.

WISDOM SPEAKS

The state of appreciation allows
the subtle realms of Sight to be seen
Seeing the whole picture
not just fragments of misunderstanding

The agreement that it is raining may be universal
and has nothing to do with the interpretation of the rain
That is strictly up to each individual

The Picture of the world
is the servant to the master interpreter
The master interpreter
is the one who determines the experience

And the master interpreter is you

The face
if covered
something great is lacking

The face
is the center of our Being
in the physical world

It is the visual recognition of our identity
holding all the senses in one area

The face is where the five truths are known
yet
I cannot see my own

❧

Words struck a chord
And started to vibrate

Vibrating to a sound that was familiar to me

A sound heard
not by my ears

A sound Seen

Through the Seeing
the message was Heard

Focus not on things
Focus on the space between things

It is a new way of seeing
mentioned in the old texts

You see a wheel spinning
However
the space where the axle
passes through the center of the wheel
is what enables it to turn

You drink water from a cup
However
the space in the cup
is what enables it to be filled

Empty space is where usefulness exists

You enjoy the sounds of music
However
the space between the notes
is what enables
the sweet sounds to be distinguished

Pay attention to the space between thoughts
Not thoughts appearing in space

Focusing on the space between thoughts
remains constant

Focusing on thoughts in the space
continues to fluctuate

The world could not be experienced
if there was no space between things and events
No space between you and the other

The cup
wheel and music
would not be useful
without space

Same is true for you

Between thoughts
Between actions and events
Between waking and sleeping
Between lifetimes
Space lives

Space is not empty
It is filled

The In-Between Space
is where life's usefulness exists

All lovers
speak with One

All religions
worship with One

All singers
sing with One

All children
play with One

In order for oneself to see
All in One
one must See oneself
in All

It is a mistake to ask the question
What must I *get* to truly live?

The focus in on the outer
which fills one up
with an impossible task

Desiring what desires cannot fulfill
Leaving no room to receive life's true gifts

Let me assure you
Desires are the fuel for the movement of life
The transportation
not the destination

Inner focus
taps into the endless reservoir of *All That Is*
The destination
not the transportation

As one wise soul said:

The question to ask is
what am I willing to give to truly live?

Don't expect others to do for you
what you need to do for yourself

You want understanding
understand yourself
You want caring
care for yourself
You want to be heard
hear yourself
You want love
love yourself

If you do not love yourself
how can another?

When you desire fulfillment from another
it is an attempt to fulfill you
without You
It will never happen
It is temporary

Because it links to the illusion associated
with the physical world

When you desire fulfillment from You
it is a certainty to fulfill you
with You
It will always happen
It is eternal

Because it links to Direct Perception associated
with Spirit World

Expecting the physical world to do
what you need to do
will always lead to disappointment

The temporary could never replace the Eternal

In the physical world
the moment of birth
invites
the moment of death

In the Spirit world
the moment of birth
invites
reentering into what *was*
is and *always will Be*

Self-Realization stems from Direct Perception
A Perception seeing the true nature of Life
Bypassing thoughts and conditions

Direct Perception of the Sacred Tree
are branches extending outward to reach for Itself
in the outer world

Self embracing Self

All experience is experiencing the same Experience:
For Self to know ItSelf

Direct Perception
however
has nothing to do with you

Let go
into the arms of your True Self
and realize
Seeing is Seen from the Unseen

⟋

SACRED REFLECTION

I am holding a cup in my hands.

What is cup?
Ceramic
What is ceramic?
Clay
What is clay?
Rock and soil
What is rock and soil?
Minerals
What is mineral?
Chemical compounds
What is chemical compound?
Molecules
What is molecule?
Atoms
What is atom?
99.9 % space, light and energetic vibration

Am I really holding a cup?

When love rises
questions fall

In silence
all is heard without words
In stillness
movement is felt without motion

This is the Divine State of Becoming

New Eyes emerge
dropping the old disguise of the personal self
Making room for the Invitation of

I AM

⚬⚬

Immortality exists within the shift of Inner Vision
from self to Self

A SACRED MOMENT:
SEEING

Do your eyes really see? When you see anything in the physical world, you are sensing and interpreting it within yourself. What you are seeing, is the interpretation of your *perceptional-frequencies* of beliefs and conditionings. The physicality is a projection of thoughts and beliefs, intensified with feelings, created from mass consciousness and individual *systems of beliefs*. These projections of beliefs are experienced and then confirmed as reality, universally and personally. Your thoughts and beliefs are projected from you, you sense it in the world, you experience it, and call it *your circumstance*.

You are continually experiencing your own creations. There is no separation of *this or that* and of *you or the other*. Separation is the illusion or the veil of *maya*. Once the veil is lifted, You, the *Seer*, the process of *Seeing*, and what is sensed and experienced, *the Seen*, are One— no distinction.

When you smell a fragrance, it is sensed and experienced internally. When you see a sunset, it is sensed and experienced internally. The nose, eyes, and all the senses are vehicles or vessels for the sensations to be experienced and interpreted by you. All sensations are sensed within you, not outside of you.

If you look out from a window and see a tree, the window is not seeing the tree, the one looking out of the window is experiencing it—*you*. Similarly, the eyes do not see. They are windows sensing the projections of your interpretations to be experienced, allowing the Sight to be Seen—within you.

Another type of seeing is when you suddenly understand something or get an insight, and you may say, "Oh, I see." This is a realization or a knowing from the Inner Eye of Intuition. This is called Direct Perception. Direction Perception lasers through the lenses of programming and beliefs and sees the True Nature of the Essence of Life: Inner Clarity. Again, this has nothing to do with the eyes.

Seeing through the windows of the eyes enables you to experience your *perceptual-frequencies* projected onto the World's Screen—the Living Picture of your life, which we call reality.

CONTEMPLATION

Close your eyes, inhale and exhale deeply for three cycles or more. When you feel settled and centered, ask yourself the question:

What kind of world do I want to see?

Is it one of love and peace? One of cooperation and wisdom? One of kindness and compassion? One of tolerance and understanding? One of safety and community? One of abundance and prosperity? One of integrity and honesty?

Next, contemplate, eyes still closed, the world you want to see. For instance, if you want love, what would it look like in your personal world: Maybe surrounded by caring, loving and/ or tolerant family members and friends, as well as your own self-love. Once you feel comfortable or have an image of what your personal world could look like, extend to the outer world: Maybe peace and cooperation between nations and/or tolerance between religions and political viewpoints. Remember, you are seeing your own perceptions. If someone is annoying at your workplace, cultivate a little tolerance and the circumstance will shift.

Once you have a few thoughts and ideas, inhale and exhale deeply, then breathe normally. Focus on the inhalation and exhalation of your breath and sit in silence for a minute or two.

JOURNAL

Slowly open your eyes. Take a few minutes and jot down some thoughts about your contemplation. Next, make two lists: one personally and one globally, or just one list, whatever you feel comfortable doing. You may write *peace in my household or workplace* under your personal list and/or *peace in my country and the world* under your global list. During the day, acknowledge moments that you can take the opportunity to perceive and respond differently in your circumstance to reinforce what you want to see in your world.

You can do this practice daily or as often as you wish: clarity and direction will surface. And continue the day with this knowledge. And embrace your mastery fearlessly, holding the wisdom that everything you see is perception originating from thoughts and beliefs. And know—*eyes do not see.*

11

THE MYSTICAL MOVEMENT OF LIFE

The Mystical Realm is where the infinite and finite mingle

Wonder is the call of the mystic
The unexpected
The beauty
The admiration
The amazement

Wonder is where the mystic lives
The temporary
The vibration of love
The fluidity
The marvel

The mystic is comfortable in the unknown
and uncomfortable in the known

The mystic always wonders about wonder
Knowing a definite answer will never be

The mystic seeks to engage with Higher Perspective
in the realm of Consciousness
And looks deeply and profoundly into the Essence of Nature

The mystic is seduced by the Presence of Unity
within All of Existence
Unity is Home
The residence of wonder

*Wonder is beyond
anything previously known or anticipated*

And the mystic is always
in the state of astonishment
by what is revealed

We are all in the state of Becoming
Even though it may feel
we are in the state of stagnation
Stagnation is the resistance to our natural state of being

Our natural state of being is in constant *letting-go mode*
Nature is the best teacher
Its laws apply to all beings

The resistance is fear
Fear of Becoming our most spectacular selves
The fear of melding with the greatest Force
Love

Take a walk in the forest
and spend some time with the trees and plants
Be mindful
All is in the state of Becoming *more than*
not *less than*
Contained in the seed
is the state of Grace
Becoming and expanding
All within the Now

Humans follow the same Law
Becoming *more than* not *less than*

Our seed is within Soul
in the state of Grace
Becoming and expanding
All within the Now

This is the true movement of life

Be moved by inspiration
Not desperation

Inspiration wakes up the slumber of wonder
Desperation puts wonder back into a deep sleep

Inspiration is love
Desperation is fear

Inspired action
is in alignment with the whole order
of existence
Cheering you on

Feel the love

This is where the extraordinary
is within the ordinary

You choose to interpret the world
That's the way it is
You choose to judge what is right and wrong
That's the way it is
You choose to create the life you are living
That's the way it is
Thoughts are focus of attraction
Feelings are focus of beliefs
That's the way it is

To see a different Life's Picture
focus has to change
I am not saying it's easy
and I am not saying it's difficult
Within every circumstance are layers of possibilities
Some easier to tap into than others

When focus is from your personal mind
the ego is holding a small flashlight with a limited view
That's the way it is
When focus is from Eternal Self
the floodlights are turned on with an expansive view
That's the way it is

Floodlights allow a glimpse
into the unknown to make it known
To receive the treasure and distribute it within your life

A glimpse seems so small
However
in the mystical world
a glimpse is the doorway to *All That Is*

Through giving is living
And living is through giving

Not the giving of things
But the giving of yourself
Adding to the tapestry of life

And being courageous enough to share your
Authentic Self

Giving creates an empty vessel
to Receive

Life can only give you
what you are willing to give it

Life's nature is reflective
It does not hold its own essence

SACRED REFLECTION

What is the movement of life?

It lies in the Mystical Realm
In the present state of Now

Nowhere to go or come from

Just the Becoming of what already Is

❦

There appears to be movement

Movement means changing location
from one place to another
We walk from here to there

Be aware of a Movement of another kind

The Earth
starts where it finishes
and finishes where it starts

It circles the Light of Sun
Bringing the journey of the seasons
All within a cyclical rhythm
All of existence follows this Rhythm

Within the start
lies the finish
And within the finish
lies the start

The moment of birth
means the moment for death

Physical existence ends where it starts
and starts where it ends

Are we going anywhere?

Stay in the state of Wonder
Wonder is from the eyes of the innocent
Seeing for the first time
Every time

Wonder is from the place of Heart
Not from the place of thought

Wonder opens to infinite dimensions of Insight
Not visible within the flat and dense dimension
of thought

Wonder
sleeps in the secret transition

Can you see the exact moment when
a flower bud becomes a blossom?
You can watch all day and all night
and still cannot pinpoint the moment of blossom
It occurs after the occurrence

This is where Wonder lives
Within surprise
mingling with admiration
of the beauty of life's workings

Wonder
admits it does not know how
what it is transitions to *what it becomes*

But marvels with bated breath
at the graceful transition

SACRED OBSERVATION ON BECOMING

She fell asleep on a large log to the sounds of an untamed river running through the dense forest. This was her attempt to escape the troubling and heavy thoughts that had been haunting her for so long—thoughts not allowing the space for her dream to grow. When she awoke, she looked up and was awestruck by the enormous cottonwood tree above her. It was snowing cotton-like fibers, holding the seeds and dancing with the breeze.

She stood up slowly and hugged the massive trunk. She felt the strength of it being grounded, yet free to reach for the sun's light. "Something maybe I should do," she thought to herself.

She sat back down and focused on one cotton-like seed gently floating to the Earth. "How does this tremendous tree come from a seed smaller than a pea?" she asked herself. For a moment, she felt grounded in the wonder and the freedom to reach beyond her troubling thoughts—a moment only.

She closed her eyes and went back to sleep.

WISDOM SPEAKS

Learn from the tree
The movement of nature is the
movement of the mystical
Always in the state of Becoming

The seed of tree holds the
Dream of tree

If all the conditions are right
especially the room to grow
the tree becomes what it already Is
Magnificent

We too
abide by this Law

The seed of desire
holds the Dream of you

Sow your dream seeds with love
And if all the conditions are right
especially the room to grow
You become what you already are

Spectacular

The mystical is not fantasy
It is more real than what we consider reality

In the present state of Consciousness
the mystical lives
In this state
one can have a peek
into the wonder and magic of life
And how the Essence of Existence operates

Buddhists call it
a *satori*
An awakening

It is the kiss of the inner and outer worlds
And the melding of
infinite and finite
spirit and human
heaven and Earth
immortality and mortality
real and unreal

Revealing
every experience
circumstance and physical manifestation
is the Absolute Self presenting
ItSelf to you
as You

The realm is not hidden
It is just that the Eyes
are not open
yet

The nature of Nature
is *Satchitananda*
Existence
Knowledge and Bliss
Wrapped in one package

The nature of Self
is very playful
And loves to play games
Hide and seek is the favorite

Here
There
And laughing lovingly that it is
neither here nor there
But plays out of Love

Self is a romantic
Self allures itself to Self
Dancing to Love's music

Dazed by sweetness
It disappears when holding on
and appears when letting go

Self gives through receiving

Play with Self
This is when Life and the player
dissolve into One

This is the nature of your Nature

Life's landscape
is vertical not horizontal

Delve deep into the layers of possibilities
through the perception of Sight

You could be standing in the midst of a windstorm
or the calm of the Eye
Both are always present

Standing in Center will present the
swirling of all possibilities
Concurrently not independently

Infinite possibilities are infinite
And live in the depths of your Consciousness
vertically

Finite possibilities are finite
And live in the shallowness of your focus
horizontally
Thus
experienced as the landscape
of your physicality

Life is the endless seeking of a horizon
Where the sky and ocean appear to meet

A horizon that could never be reached
For when you think you are close to it
a new horizon will present itself

A mystic
lives in the Mystical Realm

Questioning existence
Knowing precise answers will never surface
The mystic admits not knowing everything
However
knows what Everything Is

The mystic is the source
for Eternal Source to flow through
Using Love as the fuel of life

A mystic has no use
for dogma or guidelines
And creates along the journey

A mystic joins science and spirituality
And Sees beyond the apparent

A mystic has its focus on the Inner Self
to follow the Guidance of Greater Self

A mystic does not take life for granted
Knowing within a flash
it is gone

⌒⌒

There is Knowing of a Coming
within us all

It will transform
cleanse and be a rebirth
Nothing can stop it

It may be blocked temporarily
by defective thinking
Causing much discomfort

Eventually
surrendering to the Knowing is inevitable
While in the body or not

A Knowing
of coming Home
which has been Present all along

A SACRED MOMENT:
MYSTICAL MOVEMENT OF LIFE

The movement of life is hidden through the filters of perception and illusion. We are surrounded by the elusive movement of nature, demonstrating the true movement of existence— pay attention. A flower does not move from one flower bed to another in order to blossom. The movement or growth is in the state of Becoming: Becoming what it already is, and what it is, is already contained in the seed. The mystical movement of the flower is becoming more of *what it is*...this is growth.

Take a tomato seed for example. Place it in the soil, give it water, sun, and attention. It grows and produces a tomato. The tomato's design is in the seed. The seed contains the blueprint of possibilities for fruition. The tomato plant is in the constant state of Becoming more of what it already is, Becoming until the fruit is ready to be picked.

Humans follow the same movement of Becoming. We, too, are Becoming more of what we already are, contained in our seeds, in the Soul. We are experiencing everything we encounter, *within*, under the spell of illusion that we are moving from place to place outside of ourselves. Our seeds are in Soul, called desires. Desires hold the blueprint, and if allowed, the possibilities for manifestation will blossom. All of existence is in state of unfolding: Becoming *more than* not *less than*.

Becoming is the mystical movement of life. All of existence, from the pebble to the mountain, from the plant to the insect, from the animal to the human, from the quark of atom to the universe: Becoming what already Is.

CONTEMPLATION

Close your eyes, inhale and exhale deeply for three cycles or more. When you feel settled and centered, ask yourself the question:

What am I becoming? Is it more or less?

Am I becoming more or less of my Authentic Self? Where is my focus, is it on more or less? Do I desire more joy or less sadness? More peace or less disturbance? More strength or less weakness? More health or less sickness? More love or less fear? More money or less bills? More self-confident or less self-doubt? And most importantly, are you following your passions more, and not pushing them aside, making them less?

Next, contemplate, eyes still closed, how your actions and thoughts are becoming more or less. For instance, perhaps you desire more joy in your life. Focus on the joy you want, don't focus on having less sadness. Whatever you focus on is attracted into your circumstance. If you are focusing on having less sadness, sadness is the focus, thus, attracting sadness to your circumstance. If you desire more peace, focus on the peace, not being less disturbed. If you are focusing on being less disturbed, disturbed is the focus. Watch your language, it is a clue. Is it more or less?

Once you have a few thoughts and ideas about becoming more or less, inhale and exhale deeply, then breathe normally. Focus on the inhalation and exhalation of your breath and sit in silence for a minute or two.

JOURNAL

Slowly open your eyes. Take a few minutes and jot down some things you can do today that will support you in Becoming *more* of who you are— more of your Authentic Self.

You can do this practice daily or as often as you wish: clarity and direction will surface. Go out into the world and be aware of the *mystical movement of Life*.

12

BUTTERFLY EMERGING

We are the star seeds of Light

Embrace your human self
in all its imperfections
With the intention
always
to get closer to Eternal Self

Embrace Eternal Self
in all its perfections
With the intention
always
to get closer to You

Then you will know the precise balance
of being finite and infinite
being human and Spirit
being personal self and Absolute Self

Once the two selves
meld
spread your wings and take flight

⁓

Enlightenment
is not something you do
or even something you attain

You cannot find it by looking
What you are looking for
is looking for you
Therefore
you will only find You

Enlightenment
is the Divine Light unfolding
Blossoming Self to come forth
Emitting the sweet fragrance of the
True Nature of You

*Does a flower look for its blossom
or is the blossom what the flower already is?*

Enlightenment is an ongoing process
of enlightening and awakening experiences in one's life
revealing the Nature of Existence
Life is a verb
not a noun
Life is dynamic
not static
Once awakened
sleep is annoying

Enlightenment
is merging with the Light
until you disappear

⌒

We are all enlightened
Believe it or not
This is a huge responsibility

Many do not want to acknowledge or accept
And rather ignore the Light

Some say we are not
I say we are

However
let it be known
experiencing the Totality all at once
one would go crazy

Enlightenment is not an end result
It is a continuous investigation
granting glimpses into the infinite nature of Self
And turning those glimpses into insights

Insights to be integrated and acknowledged
in your waking state

Where are the glimpses?
Within you

Glimpses would not be possible
if we were not already enlightened
This is the reason
we strive and reach for *That*
which we already are
And some part of us knows this Secret

Enlightenment is reachable
Reaching Within

Enlightenment is the Recognition
of our True Nature
I AM Awareness

It is our natural inclination
to connect with the Greater Aspect

The Aspect of Oneness
of inclusiveness
of *All That Is*

Disclosing You
over and over again

⌒⊙⌒

Looking for love in your lover
Searching for knowledge in books
Seeking truth in the words of the wise

Where are You?

*Close your eyes and listen to breath
and beat of heart*

*There is nothing to look for
Nothing to search for
Nothing to seek*

The I AM of you is Me

Events in one's life
travel in the circumference of Self

First
events come from the projection of the individual's thoughts
feelings and beliefs
And experienced on the World's Screen
Next
the projection is sensed by the individual
Finally
what is sensed returns back to the individual
with images and sensations
And it is called reality

This is the circular returning-motion called circumstance

The Quantum Entanglement
of Seer and Seen having no distinction
And what happens with one
happens with the other

The awareness that every circumstance is projected by oneself
reveals the seed of creation
If aware of this Process
the Nature of Existence becomes apparent
Circumstance and circumference are true partners

The Seen is Seeing from the Seer

All That Is
is Self experiencing Self and returning to Self

This is called Self-Realization

SACRED OBSERVATION ON ENLIGHTENMENT

A woman who longed to experience the Essence of existence and her Godself was sitting in a garden. "I want to be enlightened and have mystical experiences," she whispered to herself.

She read books on how to open the third eye and activate the kundalini with the hope of experiencing tremendous shifts in her life. She practiced extreme austerities: fasting, being silent for days, hours of meditation, and chanting.

"What will it take to be enlightened?" she cried quietly to herself.

Always searching and seeking—always wanting. After meditating and performing *sadhana* (spiritual practices) she would look up to the sky and ask, "Where is it?"

Later that day, a friend said, "Let's go out for lunch and have some fun."

"No, no I have to meditate," the woman heavily replied.

This went on for years, this seeking and looking outside of herself for something that was already present within her. She was missing the obvious.

WISDOM SPEAKS

Enlightenment is not something to attain
It is not something to achieve
It is not outside of yourself
It is not in books
It is not in sacrifice

It is within your deepest Being
Yet
right smack in your face

An on-going process
emerging through
lightness and love
joyfulness and appreciation

In collaboration with a mind
that works with you not against you

It is intertwined with your daily life

And within each experience
no matter how mundane or extraordinary
it is showing you about You

Enlightenment is Pure Awareness
You are Pure Awareness

Lighten up and enjoy this phenomenon
called your life

Always searching

It is not in the physical form
It is in what is creating the form

It is not in the service
It is in the love creating the desire to serve

It is not in the things
It is in what you think the things will give you

It is not in the world
It is in your perspective projecting your world

It is not in the manifestation
It is in the journey

It is not in relationship to the other
It is in the relationship you have with yourself

The searching for *That*
is within You

Sit back and relax

And know
what you desire is desiring for you
to focus Within

SACRED REFLECTION

What is meditation?

*It is the waking
activity-less activity
slipping between
the spaces of thought*

*It is being lost in nothingness
only to be found*

See between your eyes
The Sight of Self

We thirst for love and peace
For its abundance was once known

Human experience allows the taste
of this timeless time
And the Third Eye
allows the image

The Third Eye is the Eye of Intuition
It is the Direct Perception from
your Higher Perspective

One Eye
merging the two physical eyes of duality
The Eye of Unity and Oneness

The Eye slicing through the thick midst of duality
and what we consider reality
Hence
the contrast between the two
Exposes the One

Life is simple
Open your eyes and look around you
Plants and animals
Insects and clouds
Sun and moon
Simply Being
Simply living

However
the human adds another dynamic
Thinking

Thinking is a force that enhances or diminishes

There is a simplicity within the beauty of complexity
Simplicity weaves through all the
intricacies of complexities

Once acknowledged
you will wonder how the obvious
was not Seen

Humans go through the trauma of complexity
only to realize life's simplicity

To experience who you are
First let me tell you
who you are not

You are not your body
You are not your personality
You are not your fears or ambitions
You are not your thoughts
You are not your mind
You are not your name's identification
What is left?
The vastness of the infinity of Divinity
To know who you are not
enables you to embrace your True Essence
Revealing the Ultimate Knowledge

When the Ultimate Knowledge is experienced
All is set in motion

Knowing *I am not*
Realizing *I AM*

Self-Realization
is Seeing Self in everything you encounter
and experiencing the True Essence of Existence

Self is *That* which is your True Nature
Pure Awareness and unconditional
Omnipresent and GodSelf
Your Origin and Destiny

It is the Self of you
acknowledging the Self in the Other
Whether it be a human or animal
plant or rock
circumstance or event

Self lives in Consciousness and Awareness
And all experience has the Face of Self

When Self recognizes itSelf
A returning motion occurs
Thus
Self-Realization

Similar to walking into a crowded room
thinking many people are surrounding you
When the lights get brighter
you realize the walls of the room are covered with mirrors
And all you are seeing is you

Seeking ceases
for you are Face to Face with Self
no matter who or what is standing in front of you

᠁

TRAITS OF A LIBERATOR

A liberator is one who is liberated. Liberation, or *moksha*, is the freedom and awareness of the *samskaras* or the programmed conditioned beliefs systems. The *samskaras* are passed down from mass and individual consciousness and lived as though they are real. Thus, a liberator is setting one free from the oppressive imprisonment and limitations of the programmed conditions of the mind.

A liberator is one who holds the sword of enlightenment
Slicing through illusion
with love as the main vision

- A liberator always has the Supreme Mentor by her or his side.
- A liberator knows that as long as you are in your human body, you *will always* be on a heroine/hero's journey, facing life's contrasts and challenges.
- A liberator does not have to control or manage others in order to be free.
- A liberator is responsible for her or his inner state of Consciousness.
- A liberator knows how to say *No*.

- A liberator knows Now is the only place to Be.
- A liberator is constantly cutting the cords of past conditionings that do not serve.
- A liberator knows thoughts before matter.
- A liberator knows perception and interpretation from beliefs and thoughts make up the world.
- A liberator knows if you want change in your world and circumstances, you must change yourself first.

- A liberator embraces both human self and Eternal Self.
- A liberator knows where the power lies.
- A liberator lives in the mystical realm where the inner and outer worlds mingle.
- A liberator lives in depth, not surface, and knows the landscape of life is vertical with infinite layers.
- A liberator knows every circumstance is the experience of Self.

- A liberator knows how to live in the *in-between* and is always working on the art of integration and balance of the worlds.
- A liberator knows everything from the atom to the far-off galaxies of the universe, holds the same Essence as You.
- A liberator knows surrendering to Eternal Source is a strength, not a weakness, and allows the Force to guide.
- A liberator has a sense of humor.
- A liberator knows enlightenment is the merging with Light and shines it onto the world.

A liberator is always expanding
with the focus on melding self and Self
And assuming the
Ultimate Authority of Creation

Spiritually there is a point of no return
Playing games of putting your head in the sand
proclaiming ignorance and carelessness
No longer work

You are confronted
to do and Be what you must

Feelings may arise simultaneously
of loss and gain
Along with a tear of letting go and acceptance

A shift of identity and purpose is in motion
Trusting other than fear

You will get no agreement from the cultural sect

This is a clue
you are heading Home

Transformation
When one expands consciously into the Unknown
one will experience moments of silence and uncertainty

This is necessary

It is the space for the Being to adjust
to the new landscape of life

A SACRED MOMENT:
EMERGING

Awakening is the breaking out of the cocoon of illusion—
the Dream of the misinterpretation of life. A life taken as
unchanging, separate, and outside of oneself. Enlightenment
or Awakening is experiencing the Light of Unity within all of
existence, lifting the veil of illusion that is blocking the Light and
separating Unity. An experience with a continuous unfolding:
a metamorphosis with a complete perception shift on how one
engages and sees the world—with the Greater Aspect always by
your side. An experience or experiences, available not only for
the selected few, but for everyone: it is our birthright. Some say
enlightenment is when one reaches perfection—we already are
in perfection. However, one must allow the deep desire to rise
and listen to the Inner Call of Unity.

Life is multidimensional with infinite possibilities at our
fingertips. Enlightenment is having a *peak-experience* along with
a *peek-experience* into the infinite with a heightened sense of
wonder. There is nothing to attain or achieve: it is allowing the
flow of Consciousness and Awareness—an on-going experiential
process. Enlightenment is being committed to the wonder and
mystery of life, knowing all of existence is Self experiencing
Self no matter what or who is in front of you. Once realized,
a *returning motion is experienced*—the Seer, the act of Seeing,
and the Seen are indivisible and you are face to face with Self in
every circumstance—hence the term, Self-Realization.

The butterfly is a constant reminder of the process of
metamorphosis or transformation. The caterpillar contains
imaginal cells, imagining becoming a butterfly. The force
becomes stronger than the original caterpillar cells. Eventually,

the butterfly cells overcome the caterpillar cells, with a burning desire to break out of the cocoon and fly. We, as humans, also contain the image of living as enlightened souls. It is beckoning us at every turn, with a burning desire to break out of the cocoon of illusion and allow our True Self to emerge, with all its beauty and Light.

CONTEMPLATION

Close your eyes, inhale and exhale deeply for three cycles or more. When you feel settled and centered, ask yourself the question:

Who am I?

Are you the personal self that is identified by your name, personality, and your daily activities and your circumstances? Or are you something more and something grander? A Self with a higher perspective. Or are you both?

Next, contemplate, eyes still closed, the question: Who Am I? Am I being who I am? Let these questions just float in your mind, embracing the two *yous*: the personal you and the Absolute You, and integrating them to be a whole Being. For example, what would it look like living your passions, making choices from the state of love, honoring yourself and others? Also, what would you look like seeing from a higher perspective, full of joy, wisdom, peace, and understanding the universal language—the vibration of love?

Once you have a few thoughts and ideas, inhale and exhale deeply, then breathe normally. Focus on the inhalation and exhalation of your breath and sit in silence for a minute or two.

JOURNAL

Slowly open your eyes. Take a few minutes and jot down some thoughts that came to you during the contemplation. Make a list of the aspects of personal self, which may include: I am a woman, a mother, a husband, a painter, teacher, finite, mortal, etc. Then make another list of your Absolute Self, which may include: eternal, awareness consciousness, witness, GodSelf, expansive perspective, loving, wisdom, immortal, patience and compassionate.

Check off the ones that are temporary or impermanent. Then check off the ones that are eternal and everlasting. Write down how to integrate both. For example, if *mother* was checked as *temporary* and *wise* was checked as *eternal,* integrate both as a *wise mother* or *mindful painter, loving teacher,* etc. And become the wonderful human you were born to be.

You can do this practice daily or as often as you wish: clarity and direction will surface. Go out into the world, break free of the cocoon of illusion and know your *butterfly is emerging.*

⌒⊙⌒

IN CLOSING:

A fulfilling life encompasses the art of integration. Integrating the human aspect and Spirit, meeting at the place of Heart, balancing the inner and outer worlds. The *Heart Writings* are a peek into the sophisticated operation of the Nature of Existence. These writings are an attempt to communicate the Love of Self and the Wonder of Life.

Hopefully, by reading the *Heart Writings* and through contemplation, you will have the opportunity to delve deeper into your Inner Being. By delving deeper within yourself, your True Self will emerge, elevating the world we all share.

-Om Shanti

GLOSSARY

Absolute Self/Eternal Source: Supreme Consciousness; *I AM* Presence; God/Goddess.

All That Is: All of existence; *Eternal Source*; God; Quantum Field; Infinite possibilities.

Conditioned world: The beliefs and attitudes shared by family, society, religion, and history that make up the belief system of mass consciousness and experienced as reality.

Dharma: The highest duty one can have to recognize the Ultimate/Eternal Truth.

Direct Perception: What we feel, see, and experience, free from subject and object relationships. And free from the duality of a "me" separate from the experience, a Perception not tainted by thought or interpretation.

Ego: The "I" that is identified with the body, mind, and senses; the personal self with likes and dislikes; the focal point of consciousness that navigates the body and personal mind through the physicality.

Enlightenment: A peak-experience into the true nature of existence and you—And lasts a lifetime.

Guru: Spiritual teacher who guides one to liberation, dispels the darkness of ignorance, and sheds the light of Knowledge. A teacher who shows the teacher in you.

Inner and Outer worlds: The Outer world is the physicality we sensed. The Inner world is where we interpret the sensations. The Outer world is temporary, the Inner world is eternal. The Outer World is where our personal self and personality live, the Inner World is where the Witness and Eternal Self live.

I AM/Divine Identity/Greater Aspect: Individual Presence of the Eternal/Absolute Self; GodSelf.

Karma: The belief that the actions we produce generate a frequency and force energy that will return to us. Cause and effect in motion in all our lifetimes.

Liberation/Liberator: A personal and direct realization of one's True Self. Total freedom (moksha) from the veil of Life's illusion. The freedom from the programming and conditionings one accumulates during lifetimes about beliefs, perceptions of reality, and cycles of rebirth (samskaras). A liberator is one who liberates oneself from the focus of ego to the focus on his or her own Divine Self.

Maya: Sanskrit word meaning the *illusion or appearance of life*. The illusion that all aspects of life are separate from you: real and permanent. When the veil of maya is lifted, one is awakened.

Matrix (Divine Matrix): The energetic and frequency grid of all of existence, connecting Everything; holding vibrational information. For example, the human matrix holds the frequencies of one's thoughts, beliefs, feelings, perceptions, and interpretations which form the physical body and circumstances.

Mystical/Mystic: The Mystical Realm is the realm where the Oneness and Unity of all existence is experienced. The mystic seeks to engage and have an intimate affair with the Higher Perspective residing in this realm and looks deeply and profoundly into the True Essence of nature. Thus, the mystery of life becomes the mystic's guru and teacher.

Observer, Witness: The Higher Perspective of all Being is referred to as Higher Self, GodSelf, or Eternal Source; witnessing all the personal self's experiences without judgement; quietly and lovingly witnessing and observing.

Origin and Destiny: We merge from the non-physical at birth (Origin) and re-emerge into the non-physical at death (Destiny). Origin and Destiny are the same Source.

Sadhana: The spiritual practice (yoga postures, meditation, study, service) to align with the Inner Self.

Sage: An extremely wise person.

Samadhi: According to the Patanjali Yoga Sutras (500 BCE), there are a few samadhi experiences. Samadhi is total absorption in Self; union with the Divine.

Samskara: Habits, patterns, impressions, mental/emotional addictions that create neuro-pathways lived within an entire lifetime, believing they are real. Belief systems from mass and individual programs and conditions. However, one can achieve *moksha*, freedom and liberation, from the samskaras.

Satchitananda: The simultaneous experience of *existence, knowledge (consciousness), and bliss* attained by the illumined mind.

Satori: A Japanese Buddhist term for awakening. In the Zen Buddhist tradition, *satori* refers to the experience of seeing into one's True Nature.

Self-Realization: The realization of the True Self within you, is the Self of all existence. Once realized, a returning motion is experienced: Self experiencing Self in all aspects of life and existence.

Self/YourSelf/ItSelf/Higher Self/True Self/GodSelf/You: Divine Consciousness that is within the individual; the higher vibration of consciousness that connects to *All That Is*, God, Quantum Field, Eternal Source, Creative Intelligence, etc.; the expansive perspective.

Soul and Spirit: Soul is the *space* for passions, inspirations, and your true identity. Spirit is the *movement* that fills the *space* for creation; the *Becoming*; the divine marriage.

That: *Tat tvam asi –Thou art That*; Divine identity. You are the Eternal; God.

Third eye: The gateway that leads to the Inner realms and consciousness; Direct Perception; intuition.

Yogi: One who practices yoga to reach liberation, Self-actualization, Self-Realization and enlightenment

Books by Stephanie Acello

Pour Me Another Cup
Mystical Writings to Illuminate Your Soul

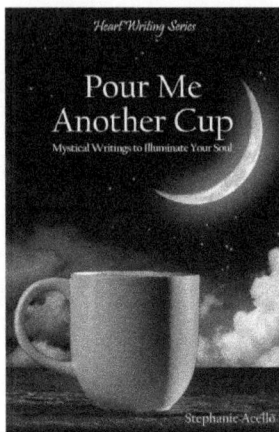

A collection of mystical poetic insights and stories called *Heart Writings*. Lighthearted, inspirational, and profound, these writings offer an invaluable guide to reestablishing your relationship with Heart and Soul.

Turn to any page and allow the transformation to take hold!

Comments and Reviews

"*…leads us on a magical journey to the home many of us have forgotten…*" – Susan B.

"*…very enlightening. This book opened me up to new perspectives…*" – LF

"*Pour Me Another Cup should be read slowly and savored, like a cup of your favorite tea.*" – SS

"*…I opened to page 78 and read "All is Well" and I can't tell you how much it comforted me! I immediately sent it in a text to my friends, who were equally soothed by it.*" – PW

To order: Stephanieacello.com or Amazon.com

Watch for upcoming books by Stephanie Acello

The Ultimate Story:
The Inner Journey Toward an Awakened Humanity

*Get ready for the most incredible story you will ever experience
… Your Life!*

Did you know that humanity's conscious evolution is a direct reflection of each one of us?

This revolutionary book takes the reader on an incredible quest for Self-Realization. Journey with the author as she shares her personal and compelling account of her conscious evolution. It exposes the most profound questions we all ask about life with simplicity and humor. You do not have to go to the Himalayan Mountains seeking the answers that are hiding in plain sight!

⌒

Heart Writing Series

Fan the Fire
Mystical Writings to Ignite Your Soul
The third in the series of *Heart Writings*

⌒

For more information on upcoming books, talks, readings, and podcasts: *stephanieacello.com*
www.facebook.com/onetonepublications/

ABOUT THE AUTHOR

Stephanie is constantly walking the path of Self-discovery, studying various practices and ideologies. Some of those practices include the principles of *Raja Yoga*. When younger, she lived within a community yoga ashram under the tutelage of a woman guru. She also participates in various intensive meditation and self-inquiry practices. The allure of her spiritual experiences is constantly cultivating the desire to continuously look deeply and profoundly into the Essence of life— an endless intimate affair.

She earned her Bachelor of Arts and Master of Science degrees in education, and taught children and adults for many years. She conducts workshops, meditations, and Heart Writing readings.

Pour Me Another Cup: *Mystical Writings to Illuminate Your Soul* was the first published volume of *Heart Writings*. *Balance the Stones: Mystical Writings to Wake Up Your Soul* is the second volume: and there will be more to come. Her writings bring the unknown into the known with dynamic, inspirational, and profound simplicity.

Stephanie lives in beautiful Colorado with her family, friends, and her animal gurus.

www.ingramcontent.com/pod-product-compliance
Lightning Source LLC
Chambersburg PA
CBHW021046090426
42738CB00006B/212